ESSENTIAL GUIDE *to* BOATING

SEAMANSHIP

A BEGINNER'S GUIDE TO SAFELY AND CONFIDENTLY NAVIGATE WATER, WEATHER, AND WINDS

SEAMANSHIP

A BEGINNER'S GUIDE TO SAFELY AND CONFIDENTLY NAVIGATE WATER, WEATHER, AND WINDS

skills institute press

Distributed By
Fox Chapel Publishing

FOX CHAPEL
PUBLISHING

© 2011 by Skills Institute Press LLC
"Essential Guide to Boating" series trademark of Skills Institute Press
Published and distributed in North America by Fox Chapel Publishing Company, Inc., East Petersburg, PA.

Seamanship is an original work, first published in 2011.

Portions of text and art previously published by and reproduced under license with Direct Holdings Americas Inc.

ISBN 978-1-56523-554-0

Library of Congress Cataloging-in-Publication Data

Seamanship.
    p. cm. -- (Essential guide to boating)
  Includes index.
  ISBN 978-1-56523-554-0
  1. Seamanship. 2. Boats and boating.
  GV777.5.S43 2011
  623.88--dc22
                        2010037616

To learn more about the other great books from Fox Chapel Publishing, or to find a retailer near you,
call toll-free 800-457-9112 or visit us at *www.FoxChapelPublishing.com*.

Note to Authors: We are always looking for talented authors to write new books.
Please send a brief letter describing your idea to Acquisition Editor,
1970 Broad Street, East Petersburg, PA 17520.

Printed in China
First printing: July 2011

Table of Contents

What You Can Learn

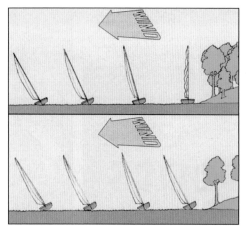

Weather, Winds, and Water, page 14

A seaman must develop a weather eye for the low-lying gray pall of an approaching fog bank, or the swirl of a swift-moving current around a buoy, or the choppy waves that signal shallow water ahead.

The Right and Easy Way, page 38

Aboard a boat, there are convenient, reliable methods for steering, navigating, provisioning a vessel, dealing with heavy weather, or even abandoning ship.

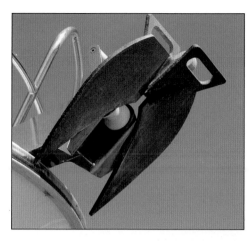

Dropping Anchor, page 76

If used properly, an anchor is a universal symbol of steadfastness and security.

Dealing with Foul Weather, page 96

Boaters need to learn to deal with bad weather before it strikes.

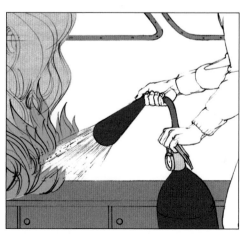

When the Worst Happens, page 116

Once an emergency has struck, the prepared seaman should know how to meet and minimize the effects of fire, system failures, and other accidents.

The Demanding Art of Seamanship

On a summer day not long ago, a Yorkshireman of my acquaintance surprised his family by arriving home towing behind his car a beautiful little 15-foot outboard motorboat. The next weekend he and his wife and their two children drove to the North Sea coast not far from Whitby. In high spirits they launched their new craft into the calm waters of a secluded cove.

A gentle breeze was blowing off the land, and by the time they were a mile or so out into the bay, the sea had risen to a lively ripple— nothing to alarm a sailor, but unsettling to these novices. They turned back, into the wind and sea, whereupon the boat began to rock disconcertingly, while a splash or two of water came aboard. Suddenly the engine stalled, and within minutes what had begun as a carefree outing became a matter of survival.

The whole family was soon so seasick that no one in the boat could try to restart the engine. They had no oars, no sail, and no idea of how to jury-rig a facsimile of either one from the gear they had aboard. At sundown the air turned cold; they had not even brought any warm clothing. Furthermore, they had nothing with which to signal for help, and they had told no one ashore that they were putting out from that lonely beach.

Twelve hours later they were picked up by a passing ship, seven or eight miles out in the ocean, cold, wet, miserable—and far wiser about the moods of the sea. In a frightening but fortunately nonfatal experience, they had learned the primary rule that pleasure, even survival, on the water depends on a combination of knowledge, preparedness, vigilance, and coolheadedness. These qualities, honed to a fine edge by constant practice, define the art of seamanship. By exercising any one of them, the Yorkshire family could have had a pleasant spin. Without them they were—almost literally—lost.

Beyond the basic tenets, seamanship is made up of the mastery of a myriad of practical details. For example, it is built on skill in handling deck equipment, particularly in the use of anchors and lines. It includes a thorough awareness of safety devices and how to use them, and it does not neglect the importance of wearing the right clothing at sea. It very definitely includes a willingness to take pains with the preparation, stowage and maintenance of unglamorous but essential pieces of equipment. Because the accessible flashlight, the well-coiled line or the spare spark plug that comes immediately to hand when needed on a windy, dark night may be vital links in a chain of actions—based on preparedness—that avert disaster.

The need for such forethought and alertness and accumulative skill stems from the fact that man is not, basically, at home on the deep. He is a land creature who has only slowly and painfully acquired the knack of getting about on water. Since prehistoric times he has voyaged forth for many reasons: to seek food, to get from one part of the land to another, to revel in the satisfaction of mastering an alien element or just to enjoy the incomparable sensation of moving across water with the free and rhythmic ease that cannot be experienced on land.

In the course of these ventures, mariners have accumulated the body of knowledge and practice that is seamanship. Its cardinal rules have guided and sustained Viking longships heading for Greenland, and Polynesian outrigger canoes crossing the Pacific. And since no piece of water large enough to accommodate a boat is altogether immune to peril, the rules apply equally to an outboard motorboat chugging through the coastal

Erroll Bruce, shown here adjusting a halyard aboard his 28-foot sloop *Kiron,* served in the Royal Navy for 34 years. His tours of duty, mostly aboard submarines, included World War II action in the North Sea and the Pacific. Since the war, Bruce has sailed in four transatlantic races, winning one as skipper of the 30-foot *Samuel Pepys.* He has also written four books on boating, edited the English yachting magazine *Motor Boat & Yachting,* and founded the Nautical Publishing Company.

waters of Yorkshire or a sailboat skimming over a Wisconsin lake.

The sea taught me a tough lesson about preparedness when I was only 19. I was then a midshipman aboard H.M.S. *Cornwall,* a cruiser on the China Station. As part of my navy duties I had handled motorboats in all kinds of weather. I had sailed in the races that midshipmen of the China Fleet used to stage in ships' boats whenever our vessels put into Hong Kong or the less well-known China port of Weihaiwei. I had even won a few races—just enough to make a young man think he knew a thing or two about sailing and seamanship. Thus, I anticipated no trouble when I set out to cruise the China coast with four other young midshipmen in a borrowed ketch, the 35-foot *Tavy II.*

So intense was my enjoyment of the balmy first night of the cruise that I scarcely left the deck. The dawn was beautiful, too. After that I went below for some sleep, leaving those on watch to get breakfast in a sand-filled cook box on deck, Chinese-junk fashion. Soon I awoke, sensing a change in conditions. The boat was pitching to a new swell from the east, while the wind held steady from the south. I tapped the barometer; it showed no change. But somehow the sky looked different, and an hour later the barometer showed a distinct drop. Such signs could mean that a typhoon—the common Pacific term for a hurricane—was forming somewhere in the China Sea.

I had never experienced a typhoon, but I knew that if there were any chance of meeting one, no sane seaman would willingly remain on open water. We turned around to run back to Hong Kong. "Secure for heavy weather," I told the other lads, "and get out that sea anchor from the forepeak." Our sea anchor was an open-ended canvas cone attached by a bridle to a line. It could be trailed out from one end of the boat or the other to slow down the vessel and keep the bow or stern to the wind. Though there seemed little likelihood that we would need it, since the wind was still no more than fresh and the gateway to the harbor stood not more than a few sailing hours away, I was taking no chances—yet.

The wind increased, as did our speed, and before the weather became too threatening we closed on Tathong Point at the entrance to Hong Kong harbor. The onshore wind, blowing against the headland, created a confused sea as the incoming waves met those echoing back from the rocks. At the same time, the funneling effect of the landforms caused a local increase in wind. A level-headed seaman would have recognized all this as the natural— and typical—result of local topography reacting with wind and sea. But in my uneasy state of mind the rising wind and waves that met us at Tathong Point suggested the typhoon was upon us. To save a few minutes and to get some shelter from the headland, I decided to sail in close, although seamanly judgment should have warned me to stand out well past the point before jibing onto the other tack for the first leg into the harbor.

"We'll jibe straight away," I ordered. I could not have made a worse decision. We turned our stern slap into a steep sea that rolled right on over the deck. The main boom had been hauled amidships for the jibe; the torrent of water pouring over the deck entwined the slack mainsheet in the steering gear. I tried to turn the ketch back on course but only succeeded in further jamming the wheel. Rushing on forward, the wave floated the cook box against a skylight, spilling the spare can of kerosene over the embers of our breakfast fire. Flames leaped up around the mainsail.

"Lower the mainsail!" I cried, hoping that its wet canvas would blanket the fire. But the wave had swirled all the lines around the mainmast into a tangled mess. "Well, cut the damned halyard!" I shouted. We all carried knives in our belts so the halyard was instantly slashed through. But it was the wrong halyard. Down came the jib instead of the main. "No, cut the main halyard!" I bellowed in rising panic. This time someone got the right line and the soaking wet canvas smothered the fire.

But we were still heading for the rocks. My eye fell on the sea anchor we had secured on deck. At least that would act as a brake, I thought, so over the side it went. But nobody watched the line as the anchor drifted away astern; a toop in the rope caught the starting handle of the auxiliary engine and whipped that overboard, too. Self-starters were then unknown, so there we were—without sails or engine, unable to steer, with a typhoon coming up astern and the waves thumping into some ugly great rocks close ahead. For a moment that seemed eternal, we drifted on toward the crashing surf.

Then the sea anchor took hold. A craft's most self-destructive force is often her own speed, and once she lies stopped in the water, her situation improves dramatically. So it was with us. The moment we realized that we were not, after all, going to be dashed against the rocks, there was a complete change of atmosphere aboard the *Tavy II*. We were all young and resilient, and more frightened than exhausted by our struggles with our own ineptitude. Now, with nothing else to go wrong, we mastered our fears and set about regaining control of our vessel.

By the time I had cut away the lines caught in the wheel, one of the crew had climbed the mast and rigged a temporary halyard. As my other three friends brought in the sea anchor and hoisted a sail, I took the wheel again. Setting a course well clear of Tathong Point, I eventually brought *Tavy II* into Hong Kong harbor to find that the typhoon had curved away, leaving only a big swell, a half gale, and a torrent of rain.

Looking back now, I can thank the typhoon that never came for teaching me so much about proper attention to both mental and material preparedness. We had all been taught long before how lines should be handled, yet our boat had become temporarily disabled

because, careless and perhaps overconfident, we had not properly stowed the halyards or correctly controlled the sea-anchor line as it ran out. We all knew that, at sea, fire can be a mortal hazard; yet we had not bothered to toss overboard the live coals from the cook box. Nor, though knowing the risk of loose and superfluous gear on deck, had we bothered to stow or lash down the box itself.

Another lesson I learned was that fear of the unknown can play havoc with one of the prime requisites of seamanship—coolheaded judgment. Without such judgment an awkward incident at sea can turn into a potentially deadly situation. Still another insight I gained was that, until tuned by experience, we tend to feel that land offers safety. And so it may. But the approach to land, as in my corner-cutting maneuver at Tathong Point, usually presents the greatest danger to men afloat—whereas, under seamanly handling, even a very small craft can safely ride out a mid-ocean gale.

Indeed, a big storm in mid-ocean can be a thrilling experience in a thoroughly seaworthy craft whose equipment is intelligently prepared and whose crew can handle it with confidence. Some years ago I was aboard the sloop *Samuel Pepys*, one of three small yachts that set out together from Bermuda bound for Newport, Rhode Island, only to sail unexpectedly into an unseasonal hurricane. In a reversal of my China Sea adventure, the storm really came, but ships and crews were prepared for it; and thus I was able to enjoy—even feel exhilarated at—some of the wilder moments.

The *Samuel Pepys* was only 30 feet long, but she had sturdy life lines, stout rigging, a full complement of winches and reliable pumps, and her sails were capable of dealing with heavy weather. Furthermore, as the storm built, our precautions were extensive. By the time wind velocity reached about 50 miles an hour, we had lowered all sail and turned to run with the wind—having set several lines, called warps, trailing out at the stern. These were designed to keep us from going so fast, as the screaming wind pressed against the bare rigging, that our nose would bury in a wave. In addition, the warps helped to break up the crests of following waves and thus keep them from crashing over us. Inside the cabin we had shored up the hatch, the hull's weakest point, with dinghy oars. Anyone in the cockpit was lashed aboard.

After dark the wind struck us with ever more violent gusts as the barometer plummeted. Around midnight the outstanding impression was of noise—the shriek of wind in the rigging and the furious hissing and crashing of the waves breaking around us. In such a situation one cannot fail to be in awe of the wild power of the sea. Yet if you have learned to roll along in time with the violence of the elements, you can actually revel in nature's display of ferocity as great waves mount up and break, while smothers of spray hurtle past you.

After some 15 hours the hurricane had passed over us, and our little vessels, lying to without sails and drifting with the storm, had survived all that turmoil with no damage. Yet a Coast Guard cutter some 10 times our size, on weather patrol in the area, suffered loss of deck equipment by steaming fast through mountainous seas to stand by us.

Equally violent weather can assail almost any lake, sea, or river. Lough Derg, a lake on the River Shannon in the middle of Ireland, is a

typically sheltered piece of inland water, some 25 miles long by 8 to 10 miles at its widest. Small motor-driven barges—and nowadays pleasure yachts too—traverse it constantly with hardly a thought of danger. Yet on December 8, 1946, a sudden storm hit the Lough, caught a barge crew unaware and drowned three of those aboard. And even on the Serpentine, the tiny, 6-to 16-foot-deep artificial lake in London's Hyde Park, wind squalls have been known to overturn rental dinghies sailed by novices—so far, fortunately, without loss of life.

The most diabolical seas I myself have ever seen were not those in mid-ocean but in a channel only seven miles wide—the Pentland Firth, which separates the Orkney Islands from the mainland of Scotland. Storms have lashed this channel to such fury that once, early in this century, a great British battleship had her bridge carried away. Simply to take a boat out into such waters in stormy weather and bring her safely back demands seamanship of the highest order. Yet into that very channel, no matter what the weather, must venture the volunteer crews of the Royal National Lifeboat Institute, in daylight or dark, responding to calls from vessels in distress.

I was for a time one of eight volunteers in a 40-foot motor lifeboat based at the tiny hamlet of Long Hope in the Orkneys. On many a wild winter's night we were among the boats called out to duty. Each of us rushed from his warm bed to the lifeboat station, and while the launchers prepared the boat, we donned oilskins and life belts, quickly but carefully. The coxswain always insisted that each of us check the adjustments of the next man's life belt and even delayed launching a minute if one man's strap was twisted. Then at his signal the boat began her skid down the steep runway.

The sea usually greeted her with a wave that raked her from bow to stern. Engines full ahead, wheel hard over, she would swing round at the touch of the coxswain, who stood upright, strapped to his tubular steel backrest. The rest of us sat grimly clinging to various parts of the pitching, rolling, plunging boat. There was no chance then to adjust a life belt; anyone who let go with even one hand as the boat rode those monstrous seas risked being flung overboard. The darkness was a devil-black obscurity that shocked the mind as spray-laden gusts bit into our cheeks. And after completing our mission we had still to make the equally perilous journey home. Every trip was a flawless exhibition of thorough preparation and expert execution.

Fear was our constant companion on those dark winter nights with the gale hurling snow, hail and spray into our faces as we searched anxiously among the waves for those in distress. Yet our fear was reasoned and controlled; it was not an enemy—as when I panicked off Hong Kong—but our friend, sharpening our senses, heightening our awareness of danger and prompting us to meet it with the quick but measured actions of true seamen.

The time to establish this prudence, these sure reflexes, is before emergencies arise. A calm day with plenty of sea room for correcting a mistake or two is a good occasion for practicing the use of, say, an oar jury-rigged as emergency steering gear aboard your powerboat—or, on a sailboat, for setting a storm trysail or simply reefing the main. The good seaman should never wait for emergencies to practice such skills.

Indeed, it goes the other way; sound seamanship often averts the need for emergency action. Simple precautions like checking out all essential gear before departure or letting someone ashore know when and where you are going can save untold hours of discomfort or danger. It is also good seamanship to be sure that someone else aboard can handle the boat should the skipper be disabled or get knocked overboard. And sometimes the soundest seaman of all may be the man who, after weighing the abilities of his boat and crew against the weather, decides to stay in port, awaiting a time when fair winds and sparkling water will provide a day of perfect pleasure.

-Erroll Bruce

CHAPTER 1:

Weather, Winds, and Water

A boatman is surrounded by an environment composed of powerful and often fickle elements—the skies above, the waters below, and the winds around him. As a sound seaman, he must develop a weather eye for the low-lying gray pall of an approaching fog bank, or the swirl of a swift-moving current around a buoy, or the choppy waves that signal shallow water ahead. He is attuned to shifts in the wind and knows how much water the tide has left under his keel. Thus forearmed, he can take full and confident advantage of a favorable current, or slide safely over a shoal at high tide, or run for harbor well ahead of a storm. Dealing with the elements, like other aspects of good seamanship, requires anticipation based on knowledge—although weather forecasting will always involve a certain amount of guesswork. Seamen condensed their observations into a rhyme: "Red sky at morning, sailors take warning. Red sky at night, sailors' delight."

Though hardly infallible, the prophecy holds true to a surprising degree, and has considerable scientific support. The dawn sun gives a rosy hue to low, moisture-bearing clouds that can threaten rain. But a reddish sunset can promise fine sailing because the dust in clear, dry air tends to filter out light of wavelengths other than red.

In the past 100 years, increasing amounts of money, skill, and energy have been devoted to weather prediction. The National Weather Service prepares regular reports for every geographic area where mariners operate. These reports are broadcast continuously and can be picked up on any small, battery-powered VHF-FM receiver. They include information on wind direction and speed, wave heights, cloud cover and visibility, the likelihood of precipitation, and the movements of high- and low-pressure centers and cold and warm fronts.

A skipper must also keep watchful eye on the behavior of the water. In a river, obviously, the main current can aid downstream traffic and impede upstream. But there are also shallows and eddies, and sometimes rapids, that must be approached with caution. Tides and currents in bays and oceans are often less obvious but they, too, hinder as well as help boaters. An ebbing tide, if badly gauged, can leave a boat stranded on a mudbank; an especially high tide can cause a careless sailor to snap off his mast on a bridge whose clearance he has misjudged. Even with published and broadcast expertise constantly available, ultimately the skipper alone must decide whether conditions warrant his casting off and heading out.

Sunset foreshadows a night of foul boating weather, as a towering thunderstorm advances with a curtain of windy rain hanging from its dark underside.

Weather, Winds, and Water

The westerly winds that keep weather moving eastward across the United States are part of the orderly pattern of global winds illustrated here. Hot air rising from the equator flows toward the poles, periodically cools, sinks and eventually moves back toward the equator. The contrary movement of these air flows results in bands of calms like those of the doldrums and the so-called horse latitudes; combined with the effects of the earth's rotation, they create bands of steady winds such as the polar easterlies, the easterly trades and the prevailing westerlies.

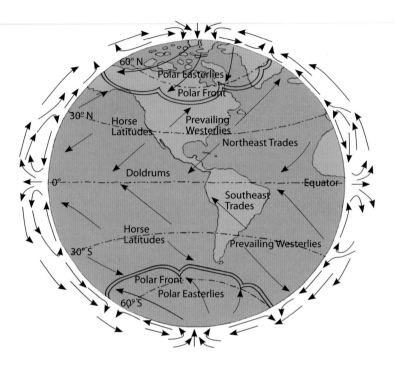

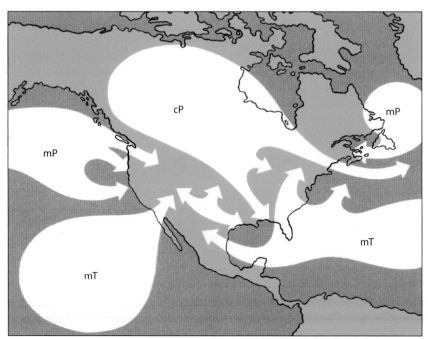

Constant processions of air masses formed over land and sea cross the boundaries of North America from north, south, and west, and then move east under the impetus of the prevailing westerlies. Weathermen's symbols—P for polar, T for tropical, m for maritime and c for continental—mark the regions in which each kind of air mass originated.

How Weather Works

The fundamental fact of a U.S. weather watcher's life is that most weather tends to come from a westerly direction. Boatmen on the lakes of Missouri keep an eye on conditions in Arizona and New Mexico to learn what is headed their way; the rain that Lake Michigan sailors had yesterday, Chesapeake Bay sailors probably will have tomorrow.

How fast they move, however, and just what they will do is not so easy to forecast. In some parts of the world, to be sure—where the trade winds blow, for instance—conditions are so stable that the same patterns recur day after day. But North America's temperate zone is overlaid by a mosaic of hot and cold air masses *(page 16)* that are in continual conflict. The area where the leading edge of one air mass bumps into another is known as a front.

Cold air is dense, and, therefore, heavy, and it tends to hug the ground. Warm air is lighter and when confronted by cold air generally rises, cools and condenses. This interplay almost always produces clouds and usually rain. It may also result in violent storms.

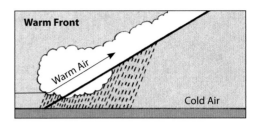

In a typical and relatively simple collision of differing atmospheric conditions, the leading edge of a mass of warm air moves with characteristic slowness as it overtakes the trailing edge of a cold air mass. Moisture in the rising air cools and condenses into precipitation. Expect foggy, soggy weather.

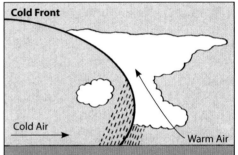

An incoming cold front travels faster and has a more violent impact than a warm front. The relatively cold and heavy air pushes up the warmer air in front of it, forcing the warm air to release its moisture as precipitation—often with wind squalls and lightning. Days of clear, cooler weather will follow.

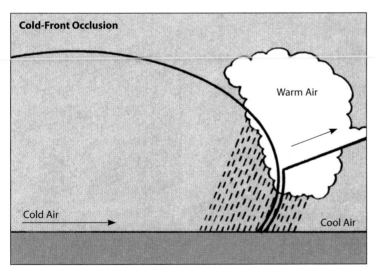

A more complex weather change, called a cold-front occlusion, takes place when a cold front overtakes and drives upward a warm air mass—and then presses on and bumps into still another air mass that is cool, but less cold than the overtaking mass. It is usually marked by light, steady rains from the warm front, followed by the strong winds and cold.

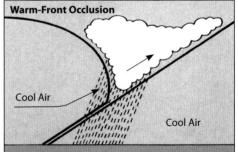

When a cold front pushes aside a body of intervening warm air and overtakes an even colder air mass, the result is called—paradoxically—a warm-front occlusion. The intervening warm mass is forced upward and so is the advancing cold front as it encounters the even colder air. This yields precipitation, followed by warmer temperatures.

Weather, Winds, and Water

Wind Patterns

The movement of air from higher to lower pressure areas—the chief cause of the planet's winds—occurs not only on a global scale, but also in tens of thousands of local situations. Although some local winds can be predicted with reasonable accuracy, generally they tend to be more capricious and sometimes stronger than, say, the trade winds that sweep over great stretches of ocean.

Where any sizable pieces of land and water adjoin, daily temperature variations can set the wind to moving—first in one direction, then in quite another.

Topographical features like mountains, steep headlands, or tall trees along a lake shore also can create wind currents, some of them baffling or even dangerous to unwary or inexpert boatmen. A good seaman, however, who has learned how local winds behave, can make them work for him. For example, he will head home before he is left drifting in the hour of calm that precedes the evening breeze from the land. And he will avoid sailing close to headlands, thus escaping both the frustration of dead air and the risk of ending up on the rocks.

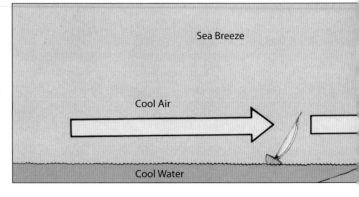

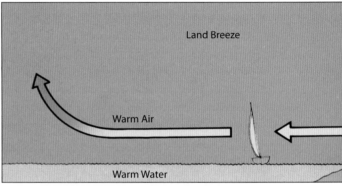

Among the most common and predictable of local winds are land-sea breeze systems like the one shown at left. During the day, land heats up faster than water. In consequence, warmed air *(red tint)* rising from the land is replaced by the heavier air of a sea breeze flowing in from over the cooler water surface. At night *(lower diagram)* the land cools more quickly than the sea. The opposite phenomenon occurs. Because the heat differential between land and sea is smaller at night, the land breeze tends to be the weaker *(thinner arrow)*.

Winds around the Compass

Early mariners gave names to persistent local winds and used them as reference points in navigation. This reproduction of the fifteenth-century Italian device called a wind rose distinguishes eight major winds, each corresponding in its direction to a cardinal point on the compass. The north wind was the *tramontana*, the wind from the Alps. Moving clockwise around the rose, other symbols denote: *greco* (NE), *levante* (E), *sirocco* (SE), *os-tro* (S), *libeccio* (SW), *ponente* (W) and *maestro* (NW).

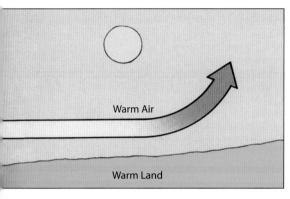

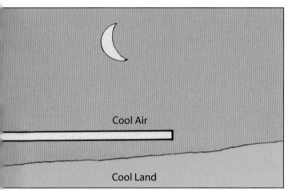

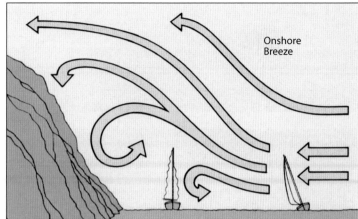

The lower levels of onshore winds are deflected downward by a steep headland, piling up at its base. Where the air descends vertically, there may be no steady wind but only quirky breezes: a sailor close to shore can find himself becalmed one moment, then pushed by an unexpected gust.

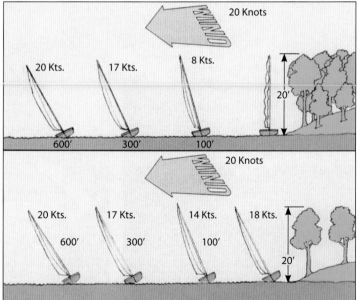

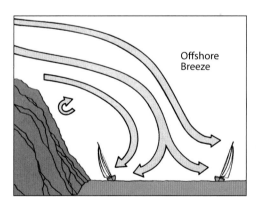

Offshore winds flowing over a cliff spill out, then down, with some currents curving back toward the escarpment. By the time they have reached the base of the cliff, light breezes can build up, and the boatman should not allow himself to be driven onshore by this reversed wind.

A barrier at the water's edge (trees—as here—or houses, or even tall marsh grass) will create an area of reduced and somewhat uneven breeze called a wind shadow, which extends out from shore for a distance of about 30 times the barrier's height. In the lee of a dense barrier *(upper drawing)*, wind speed ranges from zero near shore to full force outside the wind shadow. With a less dense barrier, the wind blows strongly near shore, loses velocity, and finally picks up speed again well offshore.

Weather, Winds, and Water

Stratus clouds occur in a solid or mottled layer, and rarely portend good weather. At ground level they become fog. A little higher, they usually bring a light drizzle—and often may hide approaching thunderheads.

Cirrus clouds always appear at high levels, and if moving in from the northwest, they usually indicate a fine day. But if a series of lower, thickening clouds follow the cirrus clouds, rain or snow is probably imminent.

Cirrocumulus clouds, sometimes arranged in patterns like the scales of a mackerel, indicate changeable weather—as recognized in an ancient couplet: "Mackerel sky, mackerel sky/Not long wet, not long dry."

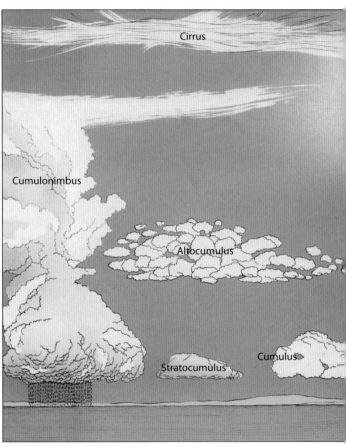

In the temperate zone across the United States, clouds occur at altitudes up to 45,000 feet—above which low temperatures prevent cloud formation. Anywhere between 16,500 and 45,000 feet are cirrus, cirrocumulus and cirrostratus. Altocumulus, altostratus and nimbostratus are usually found from 6,500 to 23,000 feet, although the latter two may build a bit higher or lower. Stratocumulus and stratus form only beneath 6,500 feet, and the latter may descend to ground level. Cumulus and cumulonimbus have bases starting below 6,500 feet; but a cumulonimbus can raise its menacing head up to 45,000 feet.

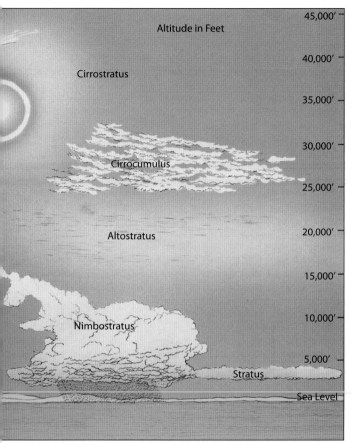

Altitude in Feet

45,000'

40,000'

Cirrostratus

35,000'

30,000'

Cirrocumulus

25,000'

Altostratus

20,000'

15,000'

10,000'

Nimbostratus

5,000'

Stratus

Sea Level

Signs in the Sky

Weather, Winds, and Water

Clouds are a sailor's visible weather bulletins. Their movement can show wind direction; their shape, height and tones suggest the nature of weather to come. Cloud messages can be complex because of the influences of seasons, wind speed, and local topography on cloud forms.

Three names describe the basic cloud shapes: cirrus, meaning wispy or feathery; stratus, meaning sheetlike; and cumulus, meaning heaped. Clouds are also described by altitude—alto, for example, usually designates a cloud at middle altitude—and by words like nimbus, meaning rain-bearing. Combinations of these terms describe distinctive clouds—like cumulonimbus, the familiar thunderhead. And each formation, as the pictures on these pages suggest, has its weather warning. Though complex when used by meteorologists, cloud language can be remarkably clear to laymen. Low clouds, for instance, are the most likely to yield unwanted gifts like rain or snow. Generally, the blacker and sharper the edge of an advancing thundercloud, the more forbidding its portent.

Mutating clouds often warn a boatman of a fast-rising local storm before his radio can. Weather broadcasts are normally updated every three to six hours; cumulus clouds mounting vertically and darkening at the lower edges as they change to cumulonimbus can bring violent rain and wind within 90 minutes.

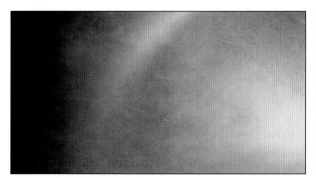

Cirrostratus is a high-altitude rain- or snow-warning cloud that can overcast the entire sky. It causes the halos around the sun or the moon—which, for good reason, are linked in folklore with the coming of bad weather.

Snow-white puffs of cumulus against a deep blue sky are a universal fair-weather sign. If they suddenly should darken and begin to build to towering heights, however, they warn of violent thunderstorms brewing.

Weather, Winds, and Water

Stormy Weather

Every sensible seaman prefers to avoid squalls—by which a sailor means the sudden, strong winds that accompany anything from a lone thunderstorm *(bottom right)* to a marching line of ministorms *(far right)*. Such ultimate terrors as waterspouts *(top right)* are too unpredictable for realistic concern; and the hurricanes that lash the Atlantic and Gulf coasts in summer and fall are almost always spotted far enough in advance to let boatmen batten down in a secure harbor well before the storm hits.

But thunderstorms, however brief, are a menace to mariners with their high winds, rain, lightning, dangerously choppy seas and occasional hail. On humid summer afternoons or whenever a cold front is reported in his area, a boatman should watch for towering cumulonimbus clouds. Cold air falling down from the peaks of the tall clouds gathers speed as it rushes toward the surface. It arrives as violent and frequent gusts of great force that change direction rapidly and unpredictably. A boatman in the path of an advancing thundercloud may not be able to get back to port before the storm strikes. But he almost always has time to put on foul weather clothes, lower his sails and close the hatches before being engulfed.

A seagoing tornado, or waterspout, is made up of spray and moisture from the air, shaped into a column by the cyclonic winds in a thunderstorm or a squall line. It can produce winds of up to 130 knots, and the extreme low pressure at its center can explode a small vessel caught in its erratic path.

The classic sign of a thunderstorm, and a clear warning to all boatmen in the vicinity, is the swiftly rising thunderhead. A thunderhead can form within an hour, and the one above, probably not much older than that, is already releasing a downpour. This storm will soon exhaust itself, but the conditions that bred it may spawn others.

An advancing squall line poses one of the most dangerous threats to a seaman. Actually a chain of thunderstorms that can stretch out as far as 500 miles, a squall line advances ahead of a cold front and brings with it winds of up to 100 knots.

Commonly, a squall line will travel at a rate of about 30 knots; but a more powerful one, moving as fast as 50 knots, can easily overtake almost any small vessel within an hour after first being sighted and can then last up to 20 hours.

Profile of a Storm System

A typical storm system, diagramed here, consists of a warm front followed in a day or two by a cold front—with a low-pressure center where the fronts join. To orient himself in respect to the system, a boatman should face the wind. The low-pressure center will always be on his right. If the barometer is falling and the wind is shifting counterclockwise, the storm center will miss the boatman at point A above. At B, however, the wind is shifting clockwise as the barometer falls, and the boatman there will be in the storm system's path.

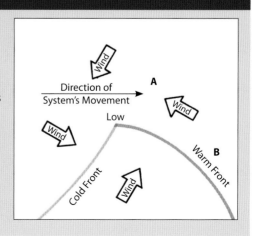

Weather, Winds, and Water

The Hazards of Fog

Fog is perhaps the most capricious hazard the seaman encounters. It can envelop him in a dense canopy such as the one, shown at right, rolling in past San Francisco's Golden Gate Bridge, or it can rise like steam from the surface of lakes and rivers. While some fogs may blow away with a strong afternoon breeze, the fogs off Newfoundland build up in May and linger, off and on, for most of the summer.

Whatever its form or duration, any fog is, basically, a cloud at ground level. It consists of tiny particles of water suspended in the air, and it occurs when the air temperature drops to a level—called the dew point—where moisture condenses.

The most common and hazardous kind of fog for a mariner builds up when warm, moist air moves across a cold surface. This so-called advection fog usually occurs in northern waters on both coasts and on the Great Lakes, especially in summer, when the air is warmer than the water. Steam fog *(opposite, top)* is usually more localized, less dense and less dangerous. But getting caught in any kind of fog is a disorienting experience, and unless a skipper has the navigational skill to operate blind, his best course, if there is fog outside, may well be to stay in port.

A Fog Forecaster

A well-equipped skipper uses this sling psychrometer to help forecast fogs. The instrument consists of two thermometers—one with a water-soaked wick tied to its bulb—mounted on a sling so it can be whirled overhead. The whirling evaporates water from the wick, lowering the wet bulb's temperature. Since the amount of evaporation depends on the dampness of the air, the skipper can use the readings on the two thermometers to calculate the dew point.

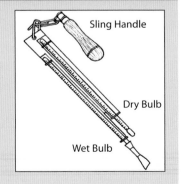

Sling Handle

Dry Bulb

Wet Bulb

Steam fog rises from a Maine pond. Such fog usually occurs in the autumn, when the water retains its summer warmth while the air has become colder. A coastal version called Arctic smoke occurs in northern latitudes when polar air meets warm coastal waters.

A dense blanket of coastal fog drifts in through the Golden Gate Bridge—as occurs almost every afternoon in spring and summer—providing a sundown spectacular for the city's landsmen, but a bothersome problem for local navigators. The fog bank-forms as moist air from the Pacific moves across cold water along the coast. The air cools to its dew point and its moisture condenses into fog.

Caught in a fog off the San Juan Islands, this sloop feels its way cautiously toward port. Ashore, bright sunshine may burn off such fog as the land heats up during the day; but at sea the sun has little effect on the blanket of mist, since the water warms less quickly than the land—so the fog may remain all day.

Mapping the Weather

A typical weather map, like the one at right, gives the national forecast for the day of publication. The small map printed next to it shows the weather of the previous day. Both of them are based on a highly detailed chart of current weather conditions prepared by the Weather Service from data supplied several times a day by some 300 local weather stations across the country.

The first weather sign a boatman should look for on his forecast map is the position of any front that might be moving into the area. Different kinds of fronts have different symbols, which are explained in an abbreviated key accompanying the map. Next he should check the map's annotated predictions of regional temperature *(dotted lines)* and precipitation. And finally he should note the letters indicating areas of high (H) and low (L) atmospheric pressure. The former assures clear, stable weather; the latter usually means bad conditions.

Another clue to atmospheric pressure found on many weather maps is isobars, lines connecting areas of equal atmospheric pressure. Their measurements are recorded in inches of mercury or units of pressure called millibars.

These weather breeders—the fronts, and high- and low-pressure areas—are in constant movement. Their velocity, however, is hard to predict. A front might speed up and arrive early, or get stalled and not come until the next day. To keep a running check on these forces in his locale, the skipper can turn to the other handy tools explained on pages 28–29.

The Weather Service map at right portrays actual weather in the lower Mississippi Valley 12 hours after the prediction time of the forecast map above. The cold front has moved slightly past New Orleans in its easterly march and is now joined to a warm front curving down into the Gulf of Mexico. Rain is steadily falling east of the Mississippi, while skies behind the front are clearing. By the end of the day the front will have carried its dirty weather to western Florida, and New Orleans will be sunny again.

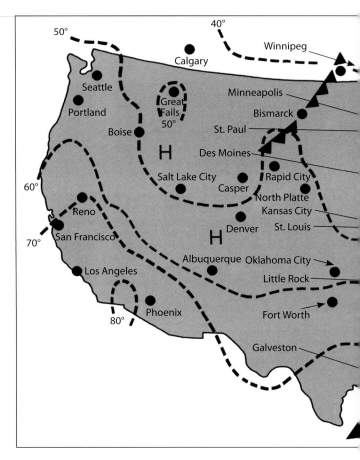

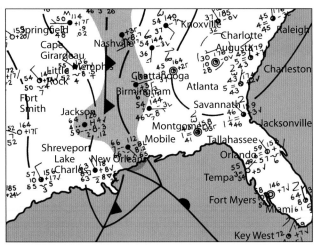

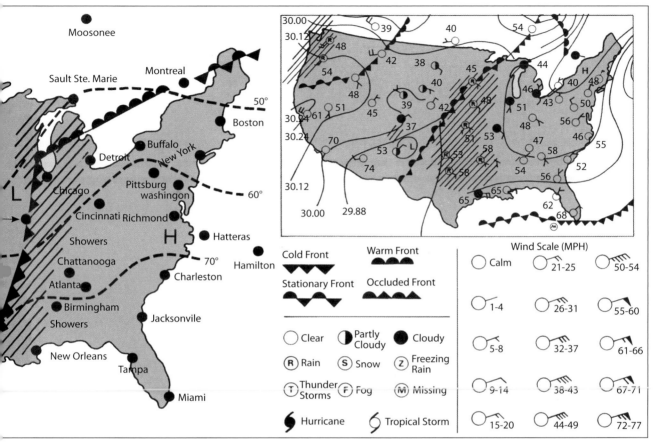

Moosonee

Sault Ste. Marie Montreal

50°

Boston

Buffalo

Detroit New York

Chicago Pittsburg washingon 60°

Cincinnati Richmond

Showers H Hatteras

Chattanooga 70° Hamilton

Atlanta Charleston

Birmingham Jacksonvile

Showers

New Orleans

Tampa

Miami

L

Cold Front ▼▼▼ **Warm Front** ⌒⌒⌒

Stationary Front ▼⌒▼ **Occluded Front** ⌒▲⌒▲

○ Clear ◐ Partly Cloudy ● Cloudy

Ⓡ Rain Ⓢ Snow Ⓩ Freezing Rain

Ⓣ Thunder Storms Ⓕ Fog Ⓜ Missing

🌀 Hurricane 🌀 Tropical Storm

Wind Scale (MPH)

○ Calm ○— 21-25 ○— 50-54

○⌐ 1-4 ○— 26-31 ○— 55-60

○— 5-8 ○— 32-37 ○— 61-66

○— 9-14 ○— 38-43 ○— 67-71

○— 15-20 ○— 44-49 ○— 72-77

This national forecast map printed in a daily newspaper on a fall day has good news for boatmen on the rivers and lakes of the Rocky Mountain states. Two prevailing high-pressure areas promise clear, dry weather. The prognosis is not so good for most Great Lakes sailors, who can expect a steady drizzle to accompany the warm front (indicated by a line of half domes) that is hovering over the lakes. Worst off are boatmen from Chicago south to New Orleans. The entire Mississippi Valley is menaced by an east-moving cold front (shown as a line of triangles) that threatens rain, wind, and thunderstorms.

Weather, Winds, and Water

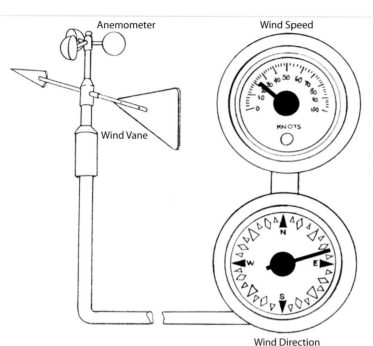

Anemometer

Wind Speed

Wind Vane

Wind Direction

Two of the most useful tools for reading weather are the anemometer and the wind vane, which are found in most yacht clubs and marinas. The vane shows wind direction, indicated on a dial with a compass face; the anemometer's cups spin in the breeze, and their rate of rotation is translated on another dial into knots of wind speed.

The barometer measures atmospheric pressure, another essential element in forecasting weather. The one at right indicates pressure on two scales: in inches of mercury, from 27.50 to 31.50; and in millibars, from 940 to 1060. The blue hand moves as pressure changes; the red hand can be set, and shows change between readings.

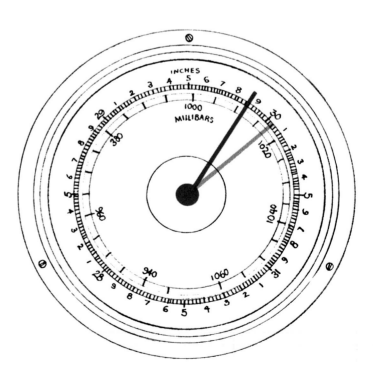

Rules of Thumb for Forecasting

To make his own forecast, the boatman can take local wind and barometer readings and apply them to the table below, which represents a composite of long-term observations of weather behavior for most of the United States. The readings need cover only present wind direction, but barometric pressures should be for at least the preceding three hours; results can be double-checked against the newspaper weather map.

Wind Direction	Barometer Reading at Sea Level	Character of Weather
SW to NW	30.10 to 30.20 and steady	Fair, with slight temperature changes for one or two days
SW to NW	30.10 to 30.20 and rising rapidly	Fair followed within two days by rain
SW to NW	30.20 and above and stationary	Continued fair with no decided temperature change
SW to NW	30.20 and above, falling slowly	Slowly rising temperature and fair for two days
S to SE	30.10 to 30.20 and falling slowly	Rain within 24 hours
S to SE	30.10 to 30.20 and falling rapidly	Wind increasing in force, with rain within 12 to 24 hours
SE to NE	30.10 to 30.20 and falling slowly	Rain in 12 to 18 hours
SE to NE	30.10 to 30.20 and falling rapidly	Increasing wind and rain within 12 hours
E to NE	30.10 and above, falling slowly	In summer, with light winds, rain may not fall for several days. In winter, rain in 24 hours
E to NE	30.10 and above and falling fast	In summer, rain probably in 12 hours. In winter, rain or snow, with increasing winds, will often set in when the barometer begins to fall and the wind begins to set in NE
SE to NE	30.00 or below and falling slowly	Rain will continue one or two days
SE to NE	30.00 or below, falling rapidly	Rain with high wind, followed within 36 hours by clearing; in winter colder
S to SW	30.00 or below and rising slowly	Clearing in a few hours and fair for several days
S to E	29.80 or below, falling rapidly	Severe storm imminent, followed in 24 hours by clearing; in winter colder
E to N	29.80 or below, falling rapidly	Severe NE gale and heavy rain; in winter, heavy snow and cold wave
Going to W	29.80 or below and rising rapidly	Clearing and colder

Weather, Winds, and Water

Weather, Winds, and Water

How to Tell the Tide

Mysterious though it may seem to the layman, the ebb and flow of the tides is as predictable and regular as the rising of the moon. Every day all around the earth the tides fill bays and estuaries—and expose harbor bulkheads like the one at right—at intervals that can be predicted down to the minute, as shown in the table opposite. And in fact, the moon itself is responsible, with a bit of help from the sun.

As the moon travels across the sky, its gravitational force pulls at the oceans, moving a bulge of water along beneath it. An equal and opposite bulge occurs on the side of the earth away from the moon. When either bulge runs into land, the water—or tide—in that area rises. Then, as the moon moves on over the land, the bulge subsides, and the tide ebbs.

In most places these two bulges cause two sets of high and low tides daily, and because of the moon's monthly progress around the earth, the tides run about 50 minutes later each day. The heights of the tides vary from place to place, depending on the shape of the bottom along the coastline and other complex factors. They also vary with the time of the month, since the gravitational pull of the sun and its relative alignment with the moon also affect the oceans. During both new and full moons, the sun and moon are directly in line and their combined force produces the so-called spring tides—fuller tides in which the water "springs up." Conversely, when the moon is in its first and

Weather-beaten pilings adorned with algae tells the range of the prevailing tides. The line where the weathering ends shows the level of the high tide. It also indicates what the tide is presently doing; if the wood above water level is wet, the tide is ebbing, but if it is comparatively dry, then the tide is on its way back in.

third quarters, the pull of sun and moon somewhat offset each other. Then there are more moderate, or neap, tides.

The regular, twice-daily sequence of tides (called semidiurnal tides) occurs along the eastern coast of the United States. In many places, however, peculiarities in the coastlines, and other factors, cause the tides to be irregular. Pensacola, Florida, may have only one set of tides a day. And the west coast of North America experiences two tide cycles daily, one much fuller than the other—listed in the tables as higher high and lower low.

Salem, Mass. 2010
Times And Heights Of High And Low Waters
October

Day	Date	High				Low			
		AM	Hgt	PM	Hgt	AM	Hgt	PM	Hgt
Friday	01	5:25	8.0	5:40	9.3	11:24	1.5		
Saturday	02	6:26	8.2	6:42	9.4	12:08	0.7	12:26	1.3
Sunday	03	7:26	8.6	7:45	9.7	1:09	0.4	1:29	0.9
Monday	04	8:25	9.2	8:46	10.0	2:08	0.1	2:30	0.3
Tuesday	05	9:21	9.8	9:45	10.3	3:04	-0.4	3:28	-0.4

Tide levels at Salem Harbor, Mass.—and the times at which they occur—are shown at left in an excerpt from the tide tables prepared by the MA Marine Trades Association. High and low tides for Friday, October 1, for example, are listed at 9.3 ft. and 1.5 ft. above mean low water. The times for each are shown, followed by the height in feet above the mean low water. (See the diagram bottom left.)

Weather, Winds, and Water

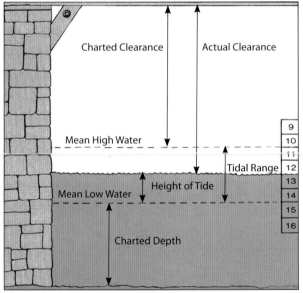

Heights of tides are calculated from mean low water—the average level of an area's low tides. The distance between this level and mean high water is the tidal range, or the amount the tide rises and falls each cycle. Water depth shown on charts is taken from mean low water to the bottom. Clearances under bridges are charted at mean high water.

Tide gauges, such as the one above, indicate the distance in feet between the surface of the water and the bottom of an overhead bridge or causeway. In this case, the gauge shows that there are roughly 14 feet of clearance; as the tide rises, the clearance—and the readings—will decrease.

The Moving Waters

Beneath the surface, the oceans of the world are never entirely still. Local winds can set water moving in temporary currents; and the steady strength of the trade winds creates intercontinental flows, like the Gulf Stream that travels from the Caribbean up the United States east coast, or the Japanese Current, which ultimately washes the California coast.

A more pervasive force, however, is the tide, whose cyclical rise and fall creates tidal currents that stir the waters of all coastal areas. As the tide rises vertically, vast quantities of water begin to surge into bays, sounds, and estuaries. Slowly gathering momentum, the water crosses over reefs and bars, covers mud and sand flats, and swirls through inlets. A tidal current reaches the height of its power and speed about halfway through the period of flood tide, and then gradually slows until, finally, the tide turns. In many areas, the current's momentum keeps some of the water flooding even after the tide has begun to ebb. But as the tide continues to go down, the currents change direction and the whole process is repeated in reverse.

A good seaman keeps a constant eye on these currents. In a favorable current, he keeps to mid-channel, where the flow is strongest. A favoring current of two knots will, over a period of four hours, carry him an additional eight nautical miles. When forced to travel against them, he stays near the sides of channels, where the flow is weakest.

Picking favorable current is not easy. Landforms such as islands, promontories, and channels can twist tidal currents into complex flows of varying speeds and directions, as

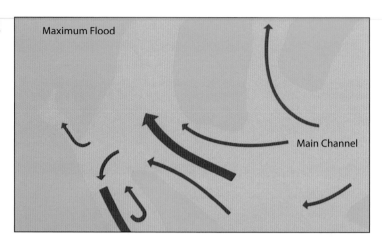

Maximum Flood

Main Channel

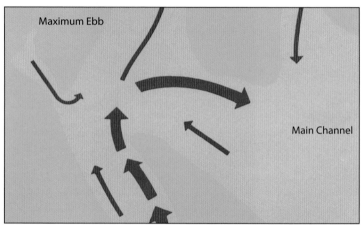

Maximum Ebb

Main Channel

The complex behavior of tidal currents is illustrated above in two simplified charts of a part of Puget Sound, Washington. One shows currents during the peak flow of flood tide; the other shows ebb tide currents some six hours later. The current's direction, or set, is affected by landforms; countercurrents and eddies tend to occur where the waters wash around a point or island. The speed, or drift, of the current is often strongest (heavy arrows) in narrow passages and is weaker *(light arrows)* in open areas.

shown in the charts above. To navigate safely and economically in tidal currents like these, a skipper should consult the National Ocean Survey's Tidal Current Tables. And he should supplement such guidance by talking to other boatmen and by observing the effects of local tidal currents on objects like pilings and buoys *(opposite, bottom)*.

Weather, Winds, and Water

The waters of a rising tide foam around the pilings of a causeway spanning a narrow New Jersey canal—evidence of a racing tidal current that would be impossible for a slow-moving boat to make any way against. In fact, a small boat could easily be pinned to the pilings by such a strong current—and possibly even be capsized.

Weather, Winds, and Water

Two views of a buoy anchored in a coastal inlet give graphic proof of a current change. In the left picture, the flooding current sweeps the buoy in its own direction, leaning it over and causing a swirl downcurrent. Four hours later the same buoy is tilted the other way by the ebbing current as it flows seaward.

These powerful waves, surging up an otherwise calm stretch of England's Severn River, are in the van of a tidal bore. This unusual current phenomenon results when an exceptionally high tide builds up against—and then sweeps over—a sand bar or other obstruction at the mouth of the river. Bores occur in a number of tidal rivers, and can reach heights of 30 feet. In 325 B.C., a bore on the Indus River scattered Alexander the Great's ships and panicked his seamen.

A whirlpool, one of the most frightening of oceanic disturbances, occurs where powerful tidal currents move rapidly over an uneven bottom or through a narrow passage. A small boat could be spun about, and possibly even capsized, by this one—which measures at least six feet across its ominous vortex—off the Brittany coast in the Gulf of Saint-Malo.

Weather, Winds, and Water

The Dangers of Waves

The most varied—and potentially hazardous—of the sea's motions are its waves. In 1966 during a North Atlantic gale, one giant wave smashed into the Italian liner *Michelangelo,* shattering windows 81 feet above the waterline.

Most waves are generated by the wind, which presses on the water's surface, causing it to undulate. These undulations march along in a regular pattern of ridges called a wave train *(below),* which may travel hundreds of miles across the open sea. Usually the wave train meets other waves moving in other directions, so most seas become hodgepodges of various wave sequences. Nevertheless, all waves behave according to basic physical laws.

If a wave is high enough, for example, strong winds will force the top of its crest to curl over and break. At sea under stormy conditions, the tops may break when wave heights reach anywhere from 15 to 25 feet. In addition, the entire wave will break whenever its height becomes too great in proportion to its length, such as when swells approach shore.

A perfectly defined sequence of waves, generated by winds far out at sea, rolls in toward shore. Usually, local winds, crosscurrents, and other wave trains cause patterns to be more erratic than this one.

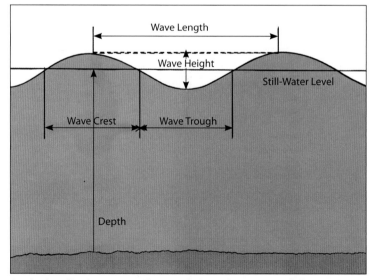

A stylized profile of a wave train illustrates the basic characteristics of all waves. Wave length is measured from the top of one crest to the top of the next; wave height is the distance from the bottom of a trough to the top of an adjacent crest. The ratio of length to height varies enormously depending on the strength of the wind and how long it has been blowing. Also the depth of the water is a factor in wave behavior: when depth is less than half the distance between crests, the waves become slower and steeper.

A wave breaking across an inlet presents a serious hazard to boatmen. Wind-driven swells roll in from the sea, begin to crest as they reach the shallow water near the inlet's mouth and break as they move through the narrow space inside the jetty in the background. Unless a skipper is skilled at maneuvering through cresting seas he should anchor outside the inlet until conditions moderate.

Weather, Winds, and Water

Confused, uncomfortable wave conditions like those above occur when the tidal current and wind direction clash. Here the tide is flooding into a bay while the wind is blowing offshore. The resulting chop looks a bit like waves caused by shallows, and might well dismay a boatman coming upon them suddenly; but though they may bounce a boat around, these waves are not dangerous.

Curls of surf breaking across an isolated patch of water are a sure sign of a sand bar or other shoal close to the surface. Even small waves will break when the water becomes shallow enough so that the lower part of the wave train drags along the bottom, causing the crests to rise up, roll over, and collapse.

CHAPTER 2:
The Right and Easy Way

Aboard a boat, there is a right way to do everything. There are convenient, reliable, energy-saving methods for steering, navigating, provisioning a vessel, dealing with heavy weather, giving orders, and even abandoning ship. And the truly able seaman is one who knows how to do things the right—and easy—way.

Among all the boatman's tasks, the most consistently demanding come under the heading of deck seamanship. These include ways to handle line, tie knots, use deck gear, and button up ship for the night. As with the other seamen's arts, deck seamanship has a common body of knowledge that makes a boatman at home on any deck—even though one boat may have slightly different equipment than the next. If a crewman can winch in a sheet and cleat it correctly on one boat, he can do so on another.

Many aspects of deck seamanship have evolved over centuries: man's quest for quick, secure knots began as soon as he started using rope. Others are more recent—the result of new equipment such as winches and jam cleats—and they demand novel techniques. Whatever its age or origin, each seamanly practice makes the everyday running of a boat efficient and safe—and as a bonus gives the craft a crisp, shipshape appearance.

The most important single aspect of deck seamanship is the mastery of rope. Powerboatmen use it primarily for mooring. Sailors are constantly using ropes, the sinews of their vessels. A boatowner must know what kind of rope is best for each of the various jobs at hand, how to keep it from unraveling and how to store it in convenient coils so the line will not twist into serpentine tangles.

In putting his lines to work, a sailor must master the basic knots, hitches, bends, and splices, with their proper applications. And he must also become familiar with the variety of mechanical line-handling devices known collectively as deck hardware: blocks to guide lines around corners, winches and tackles to trim and hoist sails, cleats and bitts to hold lines fast. Without the aid of such equipment, the seaman would be no match for the forces exerted on his vessel by wind and water.

Mountainous waves like those at right form when a strong, steady wind blows for days on end from a constant direction over a wide fetch of ocean. A 45-knot gale, for example, could build up waves 30 feet high.

The Right and Easy Way

Knowing the Ropes

Rope is the seaman's most essential tool. It tethers every vessel to a dock or mooring, or secures it to an anchor. For the man in a sailboat, ropes are, in addition, the reins that harness the wind in his sails.

The flexibility and strength of rope are astonishing. It can be made into knots, bends, and splices; it coils neatly for stowing; and yet an ordinary manila rope thinner than a man's little finger can carry a load of hundreds of pounds.

The basic structural element in virtually all rope is a collection of threadlike fibers that are twisted together into thicker components called yarns. These yarns, in turn, are twisted into strands; and the strands are either laid up (i.e., twisted once again) or else braided together, as shown at right, to form the finished rope.

Many modern boats still use hemp, manila, cotton, and linen rope. However, all natural fibers tend to rot, and most boatmen have turned to synthetics such as nylon and Dacron.

Synthetics are also considerably stronger than natural materials. Both nylon and Dacron will carry more than twice the load of a manila line of equal size. Nylon rope also will stretch up to 20 percent of its length, making it useful for docking and anchoring lines, which require elasticity. Dacron stretches very little, so it is ideal for running rigging to hold sails tautly in place.

The strongest and most long-lasting of all rope is made of steel wire, commonly used aboard powerboats for their vital steering cables, and on sailboats for such maximum-stress rigging as shrouds and stays. Halyards, too, are generally wire; their standing parts are of steel to take the heaviest strain, while the tail ends are of Dacron for easy handling.

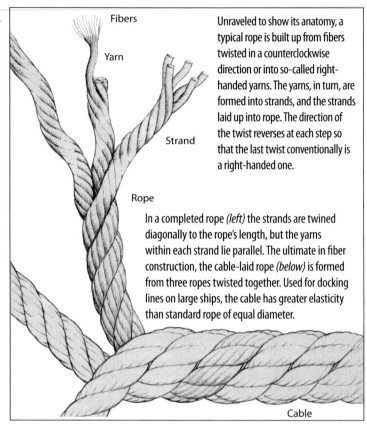

Fibers

Yarn

Strand

Rope

Cable

Unraveled to show its anatomy, a typical rope is built up from fibers twisted in a counterclockwise direction or into so-called right-handed yarns. The yarns, in turn, are formed into strands, and the strands laid up into rope. The direction of the twist reverses at each step so that the last twist conventionally is a right-handed one.

In a completed rope *(left)* the strands are twined diagonally to the rope's length, but the yarns within each strand lie parallel. The ultimate in fiber construction, the cable-laid rope *(below)* is formed from three ropes twisted together. Used for docking lines on large ships, the cable has greater elasticity than standard rope of equal diameter.

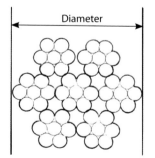

Diameter

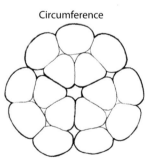

Circumference

Most yachtsmen measure rope by its diameter—though some seamen designate rope of more than one and a half inches across by its circumference *(directly above)*. Sailors measure wire ropes *(above, left)* by their diameters, with the measurements taken at the widest part of the cross section.

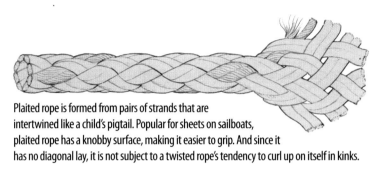

Plaited rope is formed from pairs of strands that are intertwined like a child's pigtail. Popular for sheets on sailboats, plaited rope has a knobby surface, making it easier to grip. And since it has no diagonal lay, it is not subject to a twisted rope's tendency to curl up on itself in kinks.

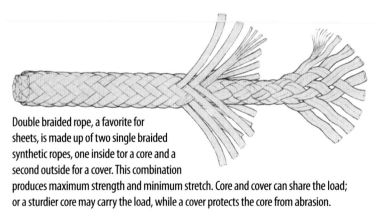

Single braided rope *(above)* is interwined like plaited rope *(top)*, but with more strands and a smoother, more uniform exterior. In this example, 24 strands are braided together in pairs. Though useful for spinnaker sheets, single braided rope is hollow in the center and flattens under tension—a trait that cause it to bind in a block or on a winch.

Double braided rope, a favorite for sheets, is made up of two single braided synthetic ropes, one inside tor a core and a second outside for a cover. This combination produces maximum strength and minimum stretch. Core and cover can share the load; or a sturdier core may carry the load, while a cover protects the core from abrasion.

Wire rope, like twisted rope, has left-laid strands twisted into right-laid rope. Wire rope may be hollow; or it may incorporate a single straight wire as a core, or an oil-saturated hemp core that lubricates the rope against rust. Manufacturers identify wire rope by the number of wires per strands and strands per rope; the example above is a 7 by 7.

The Right Rope for the Right Job

Anchor rodes	nylon
Sheets	Dacron
	manila
	linen
	wire (with rope tail)
Fender lines	Dacron
	manila
	cotton
	linen
Docking lines	nylon
	manila
Halyards	wire
	Dacron
	(prestretched)
	manila
	linen
Centerboard pennants	wire
sail boltropes	Dacron
Towlines	nylon
	manila
Steering cables	wire
Flag halyards	cotton
	linen
	manila
	Dacron
Shrouds and slays	wire
	manila
	Dacron
	(prestretched)
Life lines	Dacron
	wire (plastic-coated)
Whipping and seizing	hemp (oiled) linen
	nylon (waxed)
	manila (oiled)
	cotton (oiled)

The Right and Easy Way

Tight Finishes for Ropes

All rope ends need to be finished off to keep them from raveling. Binding up the ends—a process called whipping *(below, right)*—secures the ends of most lines. With synthetic rope, which unlays more easily than does natural fiber, the ends should first be taped and then fused with heat *(right)* before whipping.

When doubling a rope around a thimble to form a permanent eye, the end should be secured with a tight binding called a seizing *(opposite, top).* Wire is normally finished *(opposite, bottom)* with a terminal fitting attached by machine—though a homemade job can be done with bulldog clips.

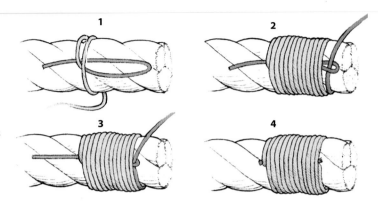

A common whipping permanently secures loose strands at the end of a rope without the use of tools. With marline or whipping twine, make a narrow loop about a half inch longer than the rope's diameter (1) and lay it lengthwise along the rope. Bind the twine tightly over the loop with turns taken against the lay of the rope, working toward the end. When the length of the whipping equals the diameter of the rope, slip the working end of the twine through the loop (2). Pull the free end of the twine (3) so that the loop carries the working end snugly under the turns. Clip off both ends close to the turns (4).

Techniques for Whipping

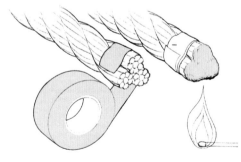

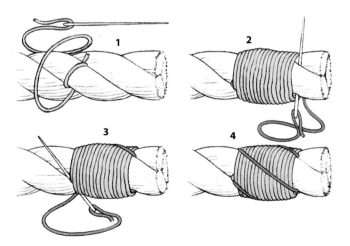

Waterproof rigger's tape, wrapped tightly around a rope against the lay *(above)*, keeps the strands from unraveling until a permanent whipping can be bound on. With new rope, apply tape on both sides of the point to be cut before the rope is severed. For fusing *(top right)*, the best tool is an electrically heated knife used by riggers; but the job can be done with a soldering iron or the flame from a match. To make a solid, blunt end, apply heat around the edges and work toward the center.

Palm-and-needle whipping makes the neatest work, but requires a sailmaker's needle and a leather palm to drive the needle through the rope. First anchor a length of waxed sail twine with a few stitches around a strand (1). Wrap the twine tightly around the rope against the lay, working toward the end. When the whip is as long as the rope's diameter (2), pass the needle under a strand so it emerges in the next groove between strands. Bring the twine back along the groove and stitch it under the next strand (3). Repeat until all grooves are filled. Then stitch the end of the twine through a strand and clip the end (4).

Seizing for a Thimble

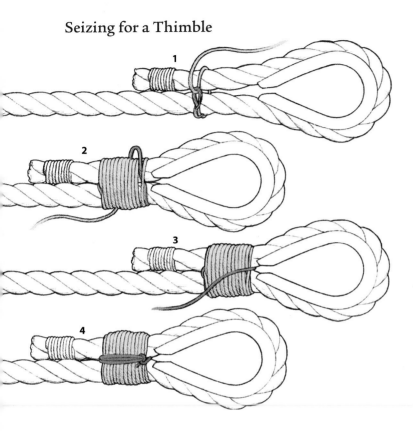

A chafeproof metal fitting called a thimble, seized into a rope end, forms a useful terminal. First make an eye in some twine by tucking the end through a few of its own strands. Then make a noose around the two rope parts by passing the end of the twine through its eye (1). Working toward the thimble, make 12 turns (2), and tuck the end under the last turn. Add a second layer of 11 so-called riding turns, working back toward the eye in the twine. Pass the end through the eye, slip it between the rope parts (3) and make a few crossing turns around the riding turns. Finish with a half hitch (4).

Eyes for Wire-Rope Ends

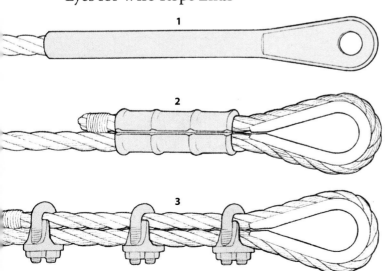

Wire terminals typically consist of eyed metal sheaths, called swages (1), which are fused around the wire's end under great heat and pressure by a special machine in a supplier's shop. Alternately, crimp-type fittings (2) may be put on either by a supplier or in a home workshop. The wire is folded back on itself and held in place by a soft metal sleeve, which is pressed around the wire by a vise. Temporary shipboard fastenings can be made with bulldog clips (3), U-shaped clips that slip over both pieces of wire and are bolted into a plate that grips them securely.

Handling Line

No boat is shipshape—or safe to operate—unless all its lines have been neatly coiled and readied for instant use. A sheet or halyard thrown down in a heap usually works itself into an unmanageable tangle that will jam in a block or fairlead when the time comes to let out or lower the sail.

All twisted rope should be put into round coils, and since most rope of this type is right laid, the loops in the coil should be made clockwise, as shown at right (left-laid rope should be coiled counterclockwise). Braided rope may be allowed to fall into figure eights. Both types of coils will prepare a line properly for either stowage or heaving.

Coiling and Throwing

To make a coil with standard, right-laid rope, take the line with the left hand about two feet from one end. With a rhythmic, sweeping motion of the right hand, feed the line into the left hand in clockwise loops about 18 inches long. With twisted rope, give each loop a slight clockwise turn to preserve the lay of the strands and cause the loops to fall into a neat coil. With braided rope, which has no dominant direction to its strands, no turn is needed; often the loops fall into figure eights which run out without tangling. Place the completed coil on deck with the working part on top so it can run free.

When heaving a line, first secure one end to a cleat. Then take a coil in your throwing hand and shift half to the other hand. Swing the throwing arm back and bring it forward with a sidearm motion, For a long throw, the motion should be more overhand to give the line height and distance; keep the other hand open and facing the direction of the throw, to allow additional line to run out. If a line is too heavy to heave, attach a messenger—a light heaving line of one-quarter-inch nylon, about 50 feet long. Secure it to the heavier line with a sheet bend (*page 52*); throw the nylon, and then pay out the heavier line.

Methods for Stowing

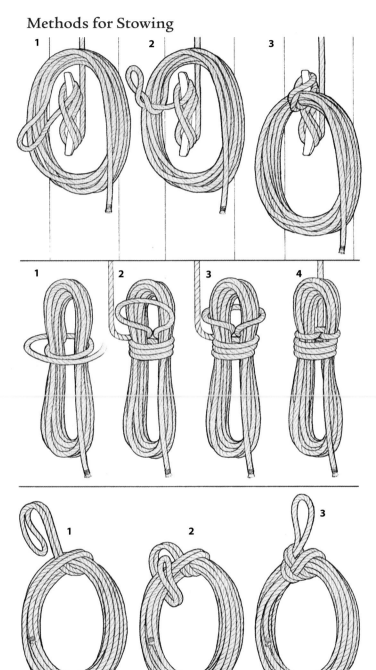

A halyard coil secures the tail of the halyard to the mast cleat after the sail is hoisted. Make a standard coil, pull the innermost loop out through the coil (1) and give the loop several left-hand turns (2). The twisted loop should be long enough to cover the bulk of line making up the coil. With the upper part of the coil laid against the cleat, bring the twisted loop up over the coil and snub it over the top of the cleat (3). When preparing to lower sail, slip the loop off the cleat and drop the coil on deck; the line will run freely.

Another method for binding up a halyard—or any other line—is the sea-gasket coil. After the coil is made up, take three or four feet of line from the back of the coil and make several crosswise turns around the coil (1), starting at the middle and working toward the head. Bring a loop of the working part out through the head of the coil above the turns (2). Slip the loop over the head of the coil and bring it down on top of the turns (3). Pull the working part to draw the loop snug (4). The coil may now be hung up by its working part with assurance that it will not come loose and accidentally unwind.

A stowing coil provides the most reliable way to secure a line that is to be put away in the rope locker. Double the end of the completed coil to form a long loop. Take a clockwise turn around the head of the coil with the loop, passing the end of the loop under its own midsection (1). Take another turn around the coil to the left of the first one (2) and tuck the end of the loop under this second turn. After both turns are pulled tight, the end of the loop stands free (3) and can be hung over a peg. As with all coils, the free end should hang down a short distance so that it does not get lost in the coil.

A bowline tied in the clew of a genoa jib holds securely despite a 2,000-pound pull that has compressed the line to half its normal diameter. Even after such strains, the bowline is readily undone.

The Knots to Know

Of all the necessary nautical skills, perhaps none is as mystifying to the novice as the tying of ropes. An almost infinite number of configurations can be made in rope yet a practical seaman can get along comfortably and safely for a lifetime by mastering only the nine basic knots and the splice shown at right.

In everyday usage most people—sailors included—refer to any interlacing of one or more pieces of rope as a knot. In its more precise nautical meaning, however, a knot is formed only when a rope is turned back and tied on itself—as in the top row at right. The fastening together of two rope ends to extend the length of line is called, technically, a bend, e.g., the double sheet bend shown at right. A configuration of rope tied around an object—which can be another rope—is a hitch *(bottom row)*. And an interweaving of one set of rope strands with another, to secure together two ropes or two parts of the same rope, is a splice *(center)*.

In choosing the right knot to use, the seaman should be guided simply by the purpose to be served. For in practice, with the exception of the splice, the various technical terms have become so blurred in meaning as to be virtually useless. For example, the so-called fisherman's bend is in fact a hitch, since it is used to hitch the rope to a ring or to a link in a chain.

The real key to the mystery of nautical knots is knowing when and where to tie each one—as explained in simplified language on the following pages. None of them is hard to master; in fact, with a modicum of practice all are remarkably easy—and useful. They share two other critical characteristics: properly made, none of them will slip or loosen on

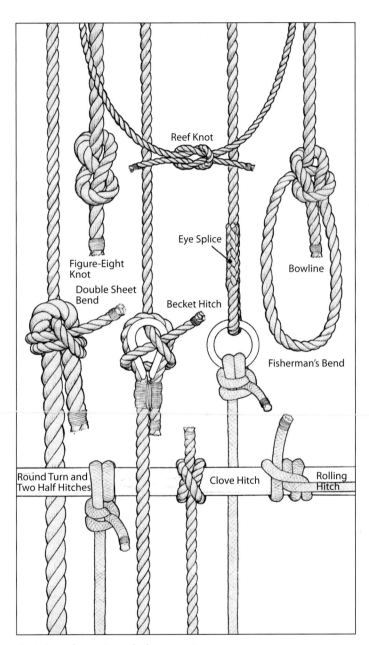

the job, and—again with the exception of the splice, which is intended to be permanent—they are all relatively easy to untie, even after being under heavy strain like the bowline at left.

47

Techniques for Tying

All of the knots shown on the following pages have certain fundamentals of structure in common. Together with a few definitions of rope parts, these fundamentals make up a simplified and useful vocabulary of knot tying as introduced at right. Once the novice understands this vocabulary it is only a small step to successful execution of the two most basic knots, the figure eight and the square, or reef, knot *(far right)*.

Of these, by far the most familiar both to boatmen and landlubbers alike is the square knot. However it is also the most unreliable. Though very useful for quickly tying together two rope ends of equal size, it is likely to slip and let go if attempted with ropes of unequal diameter. And unlike the other knots, the square knot sometimes jams on itself and becomes very hard to untie if wetted or put under heavy strain. In these latter conditions—common in storms when the knot is used for reefing—the variation shown in figure 5 at far right should be substituted.

The Vocabulary of Knots

Every knot is made up of rope parts interwoven into one or more loops. This weaving is carried out in specific over- and-under sequences. Below are the rope parts and minor variations on the basic loop that form the structure of all knots.

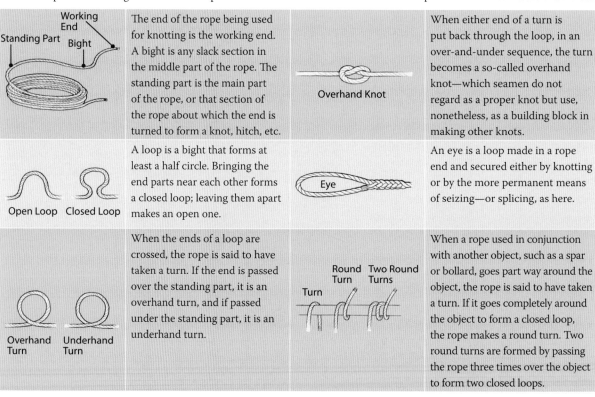

The end of the rope being used for knotting is the working end. A bight is any slack section in the middle part of the rope. The standing part is the main part of the rope, or that section of the rope about which the end is turned to form a knot, hitch, etc.

When either end of a turn is put back through the loop, in an over-and-under sequence, the turn becomes a so-called overhand knot—which seamen do not regard as a proper knot but use, nonetheless, as a building block in making other knots.

A loop is a bight that forms at least a half circle. Bringing the end parts near each other forms a closed loop; leaving them apart makes an open one.

An eye is a loop made in a rope end and secured either by knotting or by the more permanent means of seizing—or splicing, as here.

When the ends of a loop are crossed, the rope is said to have taken a turn. If the end is passed over the standing part, it is an overhand turn, and if passed under the standing part, it is an underhand turn.

When a rope used in conjunction with another object, such as a spar or bollard, goes part way around the object, the rope is said to have taken a turn. If it goes completely around the object to form a closed loop, the rope makes a round turn. Two round turns are formed by passing the rope three times over the object to form two closed loops.

The Figure Eight

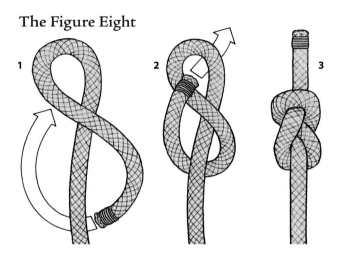

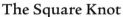

The figure-eight knot forms a solid lump in a line—either at the end or in a bight—that very effectively stops the line from running out too far through a block or fairlead. The figure eight also makes a quick temporary substitute for whipping the severed end of a line. To tie the figure eight, form an overhand loop and then take the end around and behind the standing part (1). Now pass the end up through the loop from front to back (2). To draw up, or tighten the knot, pull on both ends (3). In making a stopper, never use the overhand knot, which can jam up so tightly that it must be cut off.

The Square Knot

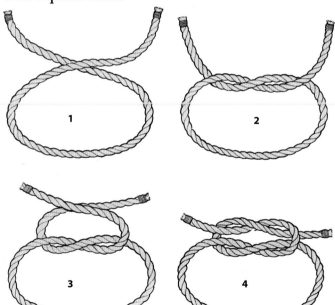

The square knot, or reef knot, is the commonest device for binding together two ends of rope to enclose an object, such as the foot of a reefed sail. To tie it, hold one end still and work with the other. Pass the working end over (1) and then around and under the other, thus forming a simple overhand knot (2). Now turn both ends back and repeat the process; working with the same end as before, place it over (3), around and under. Draw up by pulling the ends (4). If quick release is vital, make a slipped reef (5) by using a bight or half bow, rather than an end, for the final step.

The Right and Easy Way

The King of Knots

The bowline is the seaman's most reliable and useful knot. A quick, strong method for making an eye in a line, the bowline never slips or jams. It can be tied in the end of a line or in the middle, with one loop or two, depending on the situation. In fact, if a sailor were able to learn only four knots in his life, this should be one of them (the others are the square, the half hitch and the figure eight).

At right is the simplest and most reliable method for tying the basic bowline in a line's end. Below it is the bowline in a bight, tied in the middle of a line whose two ends are secured. It can also be tied near the end of a line to provide a pair of loops for hoisting someone up a mast or out of the water *(page 143)*.

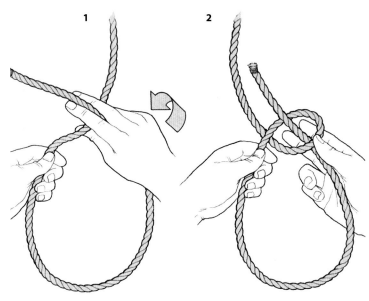

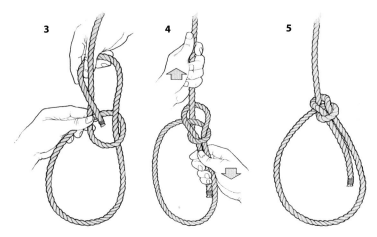

To tie a bowline, form an overhand loop; hold the junction firmly between the thumb and fingers of the right hand and turn over the right hand (1), palm up, to form a smaller loop with the working end sticking up through it (2). Hold the loop in the left hand and with the right lead the working end around behind the standing part (3), then forward and down through the small loop. The working end should finish inside the big loop, parallel to the right side. Pull down the working end and the right side of the big loop with one hand and the standing part with the other (4) to draw up the knot (5).

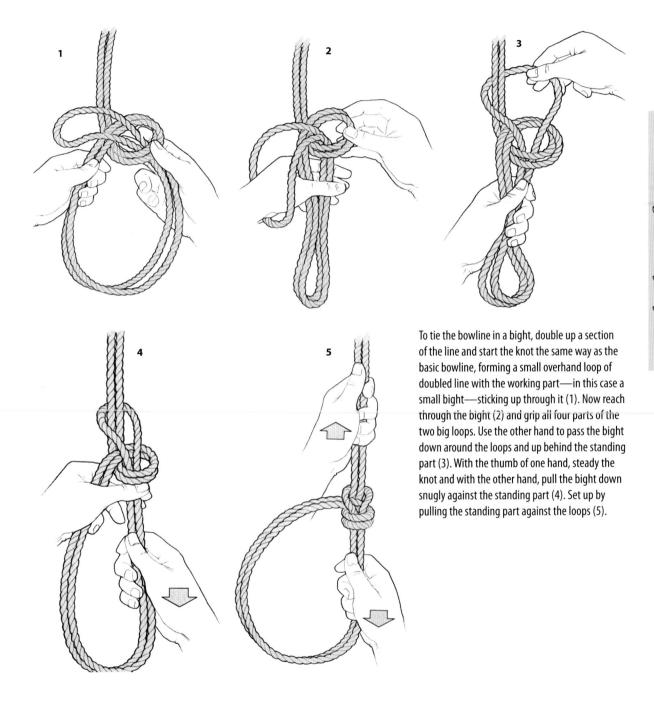

To tie the bowline in a bight, double up a section of the line and start the knot the same way as the basic bowline, forming a small overhand loop of doubled line with the working part—in this case a small bight—sticking up through it (1). Now reach through the bight (2) and grip all four parts of the two big loops. Use the other hand to pass the bight down around the loops and up behind the standing part (3). With the thumb of one hand, steady the knot and with the other hand, pull the bight down snugly against the standing part (4). Set up by pulling the standing part against the loops (5).

Tying to Lines and Rings

Every sailor should know how to secure his lines firmly to other lines—and to permanent eyes and ring fittings. The bends and hitches shown here are particularly suited to these purposes. Each is quickly tied, notably strong and reliable even under the heaviest strain. And with the exception of the fisherman's bend, each is easy to untie, even when a wet line that has been under strain is being worked with. However, because the fisherman's bend is primarily used for tying a rope to an anchor ring, security of the knot takes priority over ease of undoing.

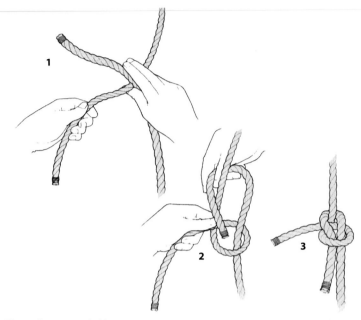

The quickest, most reliable way to tie two rope ends together—even with lines of unequal size—is by making a sheet bend using the method shown here. Cross the working end of the heavier rope over the lighter. Grasp the crossed lines as shown (1) and twist them—as in making a bowline—to form a small loop, with the end coming up through it. Pass the end around behind the standing part and back down through the loop (2). Draw up carefully and tightly (3) before putting any strain on the line.

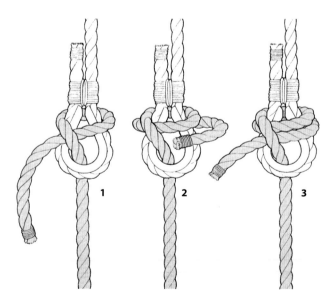

The becket hitch ties a line to a becket, i.e., any permanently closed loop. Start by passing the line end up through the becket, then take it around behind the loop and pass it back under itself (1). If the eye is large, double the hitch by taking another turn around the becket and again passing the working end under itself (2 and 3).

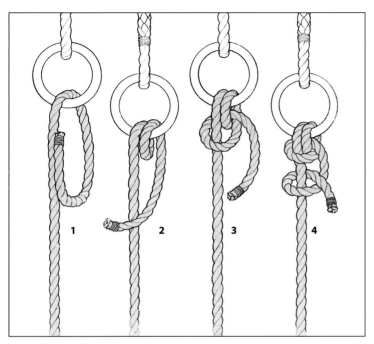

The fisherman's bend, also known as the anchor bend, is the most widely used means of tying a line onto a metal ring—often, as the alternate name implies, to an anchor ring. To tie the bend, take a round turn (1 and 2) around the ring. Pass the end through both parts of the turn (3)—in effect, putting in a half hitch—and pull tight. Secure the end with another half hitch (4).

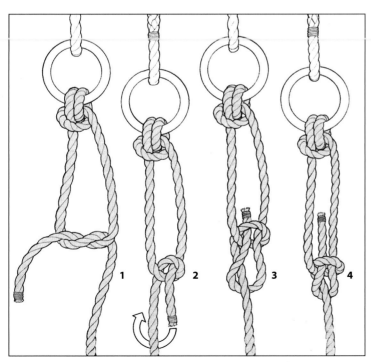

A bowline combined with a fisherman's bend gives extra security and lessens jamming during long underwater use. Instead of ending the knot with the second half hitch, take the end of the line and turn it around the standing part from front to back, forming a loop with an overhand knot at the bottom (1). Give the free end a sharp downward pull, causing the overhand knot to roll over and form a small loop in the standing part (2). Pass the free end behind the standing part and up through the loop (3), as in a regular bowline. Draw up carefully so pressure is equal on both parts and the knot is secure (4).

The Adaptable Hitch

The most convenient and versatile way to tie a rope to any object, whether a spar, rail, bollard, or shroud, is the hitch. Hitches are of two main types: those that effectively resist a pull parallel to the object and those that resist a perpendicular strain. Both come into daily use aboard ship for suspending weights, docking, or cleating. The basic conformation in all hitches is the single hitch, which is not a true knot in itself but a building block or security turn in other knots.

Two half hitches form the best quick-tying knot for suspending a weight perpendicularly from a rail. To tie it, take a round turn (1), bring the end in front of the standing part and through the loop in a half hitch (2). Then make a second half hitch (3); draw tight (4).

A rolling hitch is often used to secure the safety line of a bosun's chair to a mast, for the knot holds firm when the strain on the standing part is parallel to the object to which it is tied. Moreover, it is most effective on a smooth surface. To tie the basic rolling hitch, take two turns around the object (1). Bring the end up and over the turns; make another turn at the top and pass the end back under itself in a single hitch (2). Push the turns together and draw the knot tight (3). Strain on the standing part (4) will now force the diagonal to roll over and the knot's grip will be tightened.

An alternate version of the rolling hitch—called a stopper by some sailors—is used for tying a weight to another line such as a wire shroud, which offers less surface for the knot to grip. Begin by taking a round turn (1), but ensure that the second part of the turn runs above the first to nip it against the shroud. Next take the end around the shroud again, and over the standing part again (2) . Finish by tucking the end under in a single hitch. Set up carefully, pushing the turns together and drawing up tight (3), before placing strain on the line (4).

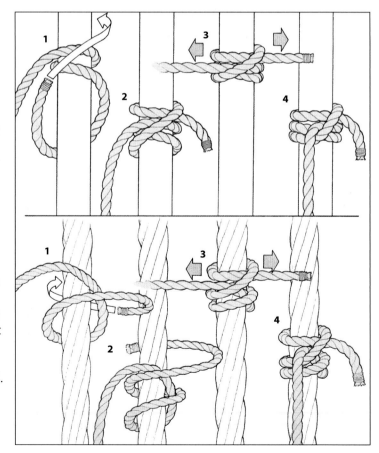

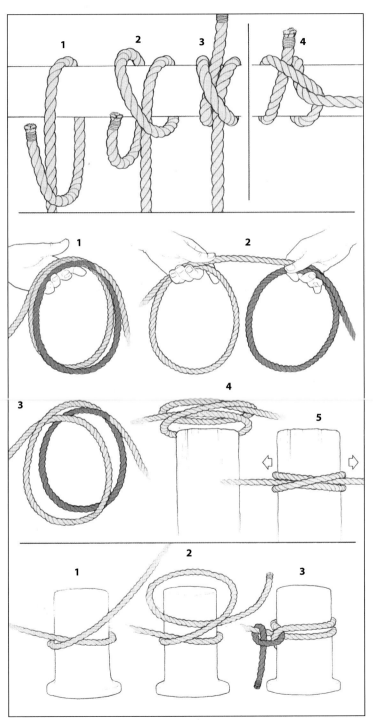

The easy-tying clove hitch, which holds well under a steady strain perpendicular to the object on which it is tied, is perfect as a quick mooring knot, whether to a rail *(left)* or to a bollard (center and bottom diagrams). To tie the clove hitch to a rail, take one turn (1) and then make a second that crosses the standing part (2). Pass the end up under the second turn in a single hitch (3). Note, however, that the knot begins to come undone under a sideways strain (4).

When a boat's crew wants to make a quick fastening to a bollard or piling, the best knot is a clove hitch tied in hand, that is, completed loosely before being dropped over the object. To tie the clove hitch in the hand, take two loops in the left hand (1); pass the second loop around behind the first (2 and 3), thus forming both an overhand and an underhand loop. Slip both loops over the bollard (4) and tighten the knot with even pressure on both ends (5). This method is particularly convenient when a boat whose lines have no eyes is temporarily docked.

When standing on a dock and handling a bow or stern line with no eye, use this method of tying the clove hitch to secure the vessel. Upon catching the line, take an underhand turn around the bollard or piling (1). If the boat is still moving, hold the line hard with this turn to snub the craft to a stop. Then make a second underhand loop and drop it over the object (2). For extra insurance, finish off the clove with a half hitch around the line's standing part (3).

A Permanent Eye

The best way to form a permanent loop in a dock line or any other piece of rope is by making an eye splice. And though rope manufacturers provide line with ready-made splices, many sailors avoid the size limitations and costs by making their own.

It takes no more than 20 minutes to splice a fiber or nylon line of standard three-strand, half-inch rope, such as that shown at right. The loop can be tailored to the size of the cleats and bollards most likely to be encountered.

When finished, a splice barely weakens the line at all: 5 to 10 percent compared to the 30 to 40 percent of a bowline *(pages 50–51)*. Finally, the splice is particularly satisfying to make. Even the most seasoned sailors take pride in their splices, often tapering them by progressively trimming fibers off the strands as they weave.

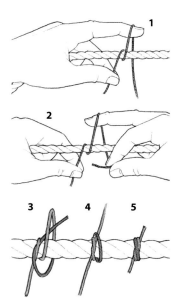

To tie a constrictor, use whipping cord and take two turns around the strand, holding the second turn open with the left index finger (1). Take the working end between the right thumb and index finger, transfer the loop to the right middle finger (2) and pass the working end through both turns (3). Tighten from both ends (4, 5), easing the second turn down to bind the first.

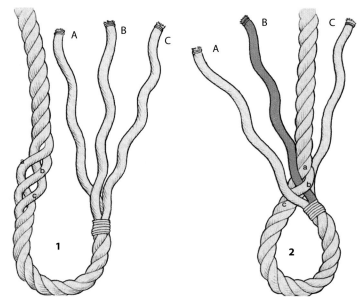

(1) Whip the rope about eight inches from the end and unlay the strands A, B, and C. Whip each strand end (left). Form an eye and open up the strands a, b, and c in the standing part. (2) Lay the working end over the standing part with A on top and to the left. Tuck B under b, from right to left, and pull it through.

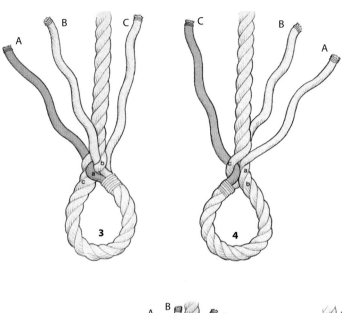

(3) Bring A over b, tuck it under a, and pull it through until its tension matches that on B. As you work, maintain the lay of the strands by twisting each clockwise as you pull it through. (4) Turn the splice over and tuck the final strand, C, under c, from right to left. Tucks are always taken from right to left, against the lay of the rope.

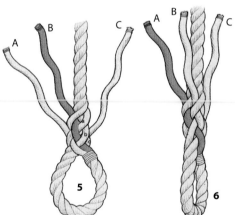

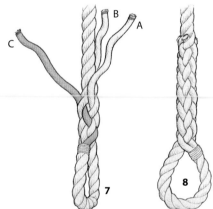

(5) Turn the splice over again; lay B over a and tuck it under the next strand. Continue the process (6) with A and—rotating the splice—with strand C (7), passing each strand in turn over one strand in the standing part and tucking it under the next. As you rotate, pull and twist each strand in sequence to maintain even tension and lay.

To finish, in natural fiber continue for at least three more tucks; use five more tucks in synthetics. Then cut off the ends. With fiber, leave half-inch tag ends, which will work themselves back in and hold. With synthetics, fuse the ends to prevent them from slipping out. Roll the finished splice (8) in the hands or underfoot to even it out.

The Right and Easy Way

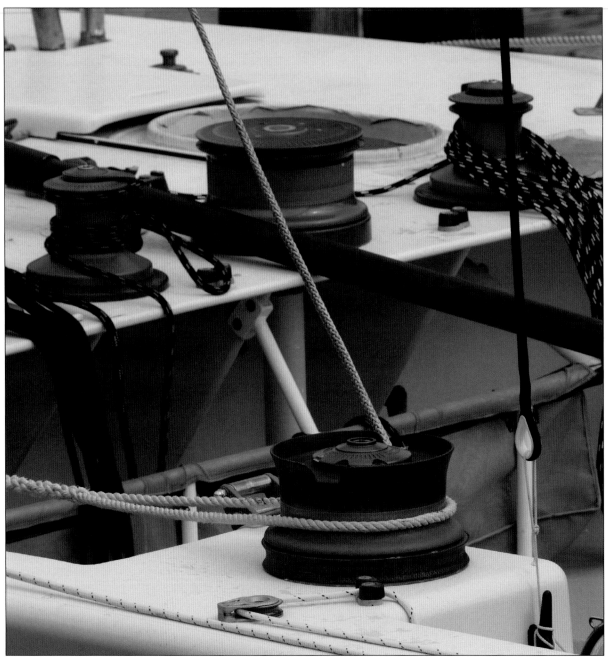

Winches and attendant deck gear stand at the ready on an America's
Cup racing yacht.

The Essential Deck Gear

The gleaming winches, cleats, blocks, and fairleads shown at left are as essential as an engine or sails in making the vessel go. These simple yet ingenious devices, known collectively as deck hardware. Fairleads guide the lines along the deck; blocks are seagoing pulleys that allow the lines to turn sharp corners; winches make lines easier to haul; and cleats secure the ends of lines to the boat.

Even the most modest outboard runabout normally carries three cleats: one in the bow for attaching a docking or anchor line and one on each quarter for other docking lines from the stern. A sailboat, with its complement of halyards, sheets, outhauls, and downhauls, requires more complex deck hardware. The very smallest needs a cleat for holding the main halyard, and on most vessels a cleat secures every other piece of running rigging.

On a large sailing craft, where the pressure of wind against the sails may run to thousands of pounds, winches are indispensable for providing the mechanical advantage needed to control the sheets and heavy sails. On most sailboats, fairleads amidships near either rail direct the jib sheets aft, while additional fairleads may guide other elements of the running rigging to their proper winches and cleats.

To withstand the tensions of hard sailing, all deck hardware should be securely mounted with through-deck bolts and constructed of sturdy, corrosion-resistant material. Cleats and winches may be of stainless steel, lightweight aluminum, or long-lasting marine bronze—or a combination of several metals. Blocks may be

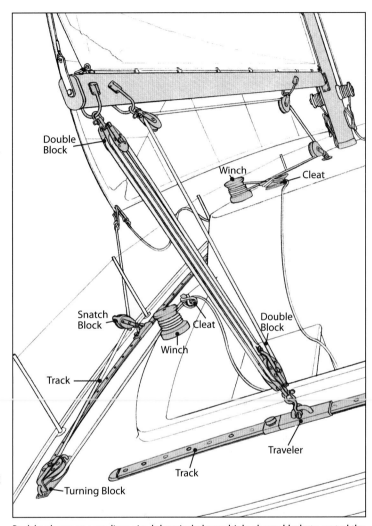

Deck hardware on a medium-sized sloop includes multiple-sheave blocks to control the mainsheet, whose position can be adjusted along a track by a slide called a traveler. The jib sheet leads through a snatch block on another track and through a turning block on the stern. Both sheets run to winches and secure on convenient cleats.

made of varnished wood with bronze or steel fittings, or they may be of metal, or of a light, tough, high-tensile plastic. Some yachtsmen lavish enormous sums on deck equipment. But for the boatman on a 26-foot cruiser, a reasonable amount will buy all the deck hardware necessary to put his lines to work.

The Right and Easy Way

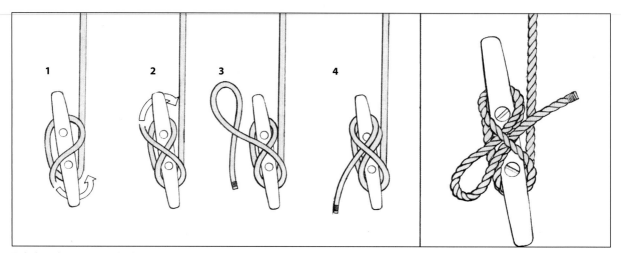

To belay a line to a standard cleat, wrap it once around the cleat's base (1), then lead it over the top of the cleat and around the lower horn (2) to form a figure eight. Make one more figure eight and finish with an underhand loop (3), which is passed over the upper horn to form a half hitch (4). The half hitch may be made with a half bow *(far right)* for quick release. When cleating sheets, some boatmen omit the half hitch and finish with a turn around the cleat's base.

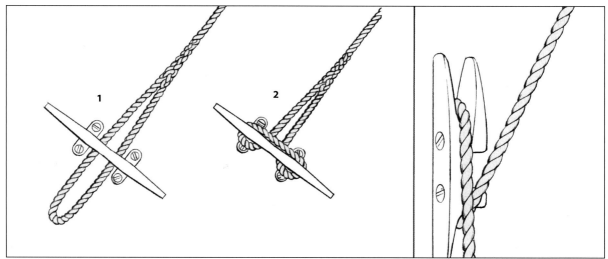

Most mooring cleats are open at the base to allow the spliced-in loops of mooring lines to be made fast easily. To do so, feed the eye through the opening (1), then loop it back over both horns and pull the line taut (2). Another eye can be looped to the same cleat if led through from the opposite direction.

In belaying a line to a jam cleat, first lead the line under the open horn, then inside the sharp V of the jam. Pull the line firmly toward you so that it wedges securely between the horn and the base. While jam cleats are fast and easy to use, they tend to chafe a line and thus may tend to shorten its life.

Cleats for Belaying

A stout cleat provides a quick, sure way to make fast a line—and hold it, no matter how great the strain. The commonest cleat, used for holding down anything from a mainsheet to a mooring line, consists of two arms, or horns, attached to a base, which should be screwed or bolted to the boat. A line being secured to a standard cleat is wrapped, or belayed, in a series of figure eights *(left)*.

A good seaman can belay a line on a standard cleat in two or three seconds. But specialized, fast-acting cleats developed for racing make belaying virtually instantaneous. Jam cleats snag the line in a sharp V under one arm, or horn *(left, bottom)*, and cam cleats grip the line between two swiveling serrated jaws *(right)*. Both cam and jam cleats release a line just as quickly—making them useful for main-sheets and jib sheets, which demand frequent adjusting.

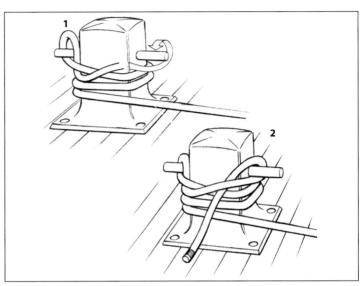

When belaying to a bitt, begin by taking several turns around the base of the post below the metal crosspiece. Then make a half hitch around one pin by slipping an underhand loop over its end (1). Finish by slipping a second underhand loop over the other pin and pulling the line tight (2).

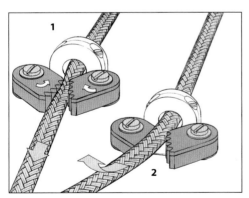

To make fast with a cam cleat, haul the line over the center of the cleat (1) and press it down against the tops of the spring-loaded cams, spreading them apart so the line drops between them. When the cams swivel back *(small arrows)* they bite the line and hold it. To let go the line (2), tug it back and upward.

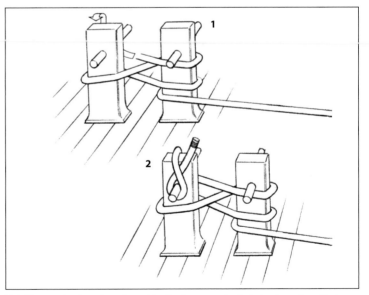

Twin bitts, used on large boats for making fast hawsers, take the belay shown here. First make a complete turn around the near bitt; then make a figure eight around both bitts (1). Finish off on either bitt by directing the line under one pin and over the bitt top (2); slip a half hitch over the opposite pin.

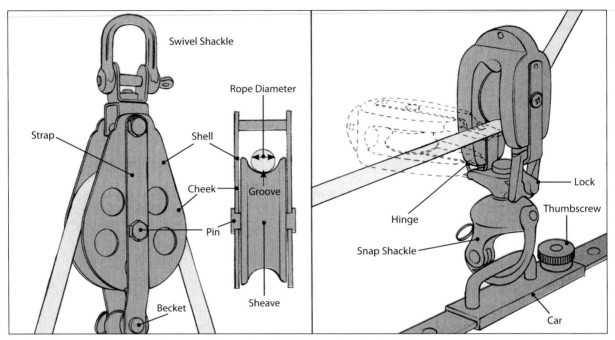

Swivel Shackle

Rope Diameter

Strap

Shell

Cheek

Groove

Pin

Becket

Sheave

Lock

Thumbscrew

Hinge

Snap Shackle

Car

A typical block consists of a grooved sheave, which is encased in a shell of metal or plastic cheeks reinforced by metal straps. The sheave turns on a pin that runs through the cheeks. The block is attached by a swivel shackle at one end; another fastening device, called a becket, is built into the opposite end.

A snatch block has a hinged shell, which opens up so that a line can be set inside without having to reeve it through from one end. Often used to control the lead of a jib sheet *(above, right)*, the block is commonly shackled to a slide, or car, which can be positioned along a track.

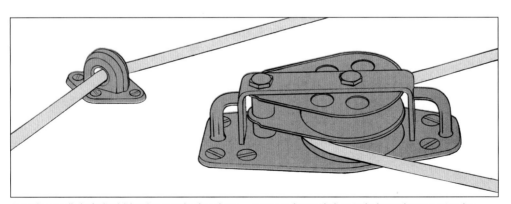

A simple eye called a fairlead *(above)* may guide a line along a deck, and even bend it through small turns. Sharp turns demand a turning block, like the double-sheaved block above. Typically fitted to a boat's quarter, as at right, this block accommodates a jib sheet in the lower sheave, a spinnaker sheet in the upper one. Turning blocks can redirect a line through a 180° angle, but must be strong and be solidly bolted, since a sharp turn doubles the strain on the block.

Blocks and Tackles

To direct the lines aboard his boat around corners, and for greater ease in hauling on those lines, every boatman makes regular use of blocks and tackles. Each block consists of one or more pulleys, or sheaves, mounted on an axle. The single block *(opposite, left)* has one sheave for a single line; a double block *(opposite, bottom)* with two sheaves will accommodate two lines simultaneously.

A line running through two or more blocks rigged opposite each other forms a tackle (boatmen pronounce it *tayckle*), a device that increases the force applicable to an object—such as a boom that must be hauled in *(below)*. At its simplest a tackle consists of two single blocks, one fixed, the other attached to the object to be moved. A line runs from the becket of one block, through the sheave in the second block and back around the first block. The object's weight is thus distributed between the multiple sections of line, and the mechanical advantage is determined by the number of lines that run from the moving block.

For example, the mechanical advantage of the handy-billy at right can be either 3 or 4 to 1—with the added convenience of a lead directly to a cam cleat on the lower block. Even allowing for loss of efficiency due to friction, this tackle adds plenty of heft for such shipboard tasks as heaving up a fouled anchor.

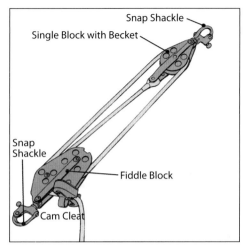

An all-purpose portable tackle called a handy-billy, often used to hold down the boom *(bottom)*, is made up of one single block and one specialized double block, called a fiddle block. Snap shackles at either end allow quick attachment, and a cam cleat on the fiddle block locks the line. In action, if the double block is fixed, the handy-billy provides a mechanical advantage of 3 to 7; if the double block moves and the single block is fixed, the pull becomes 4 to 1.

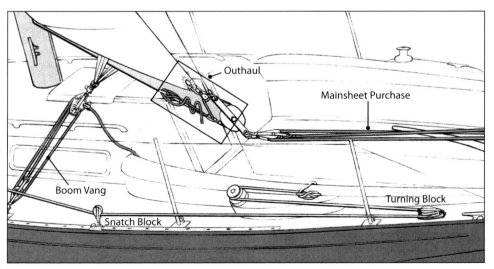

Tackles attached to the boom of this craft control both the trim of the boom and the shape of the sail. A single block on the boom and a double block on the afterdeck adjust the mainsheet. A handy-billy serves as a boom vang, which prevents the boom from spilling wind from the sail on a leeward course, and also protects against an accidental jibe. The outhaul, doubled back from the clew of the mainsail to the end of the boom, adjusts tension along the sail's foot.

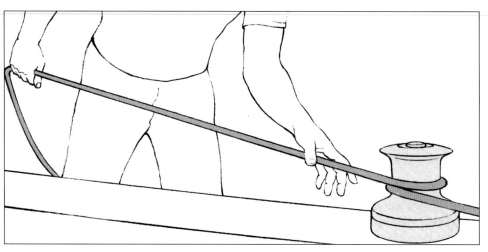

To use a drum winch, stand behind it (away from the strain in the line) and start by taking one turn around the drum. Always wrap the line clockwise—the direction in which winches are designed to work. Then haul in, or tail, the line briskly, tossing the excess behind you. Stop when you feel resistance.

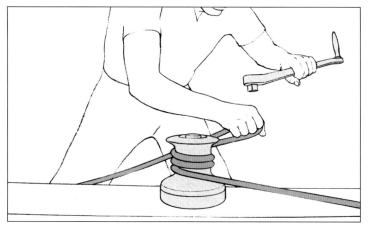

Holding the tail firmly, take two or three quick turns around the winch. Experience will show how many turns to take; too few and the line may slip, too many may cause overrides. Prepare to insert the crank, grasping it by the middle so the locking device can be cleanly inserted into the drum.

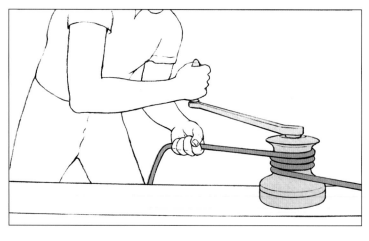

Start cranking with one hand and keep tension on the tail with the other. Lines under great strain—genoa sheets, for example—may require a second crew member to maintain sufficient tension on the tail. When the sail is properly trimmed, belay the tail to a cleat and remove the winch handle.

Winches at Work

Winches, like tackles, are a means for multiplying the force applicable to a line. But where shipboard tackles normally provide a mechanical advantage of no better than 4 to 1, a winch can achieve advantages of up to 60 to 1.

A standard deck winch, like the drum winch at left, consists of a base, a drum, a central shaft, and a cranking handle. However, on a modern craft, winches can vary enormously in size and function. Between extremes, different combinations of drum size, handle length, and gearing provide a power ratio to suit every shipboard need. Drum winches are most often used for sheets that must be cast off quickly.

On the reel winch *(right),* primarily used for raising sails that have wire halyards, the entire line winds onto the drum; and a brake locks the winch to keep the sail up.

Using a winch is not difficult, but it requires some care. On a drum winch, for example, if the working part of the line rides over the upper turns, the winch can jam. And sloppy handling can be very dangerous.

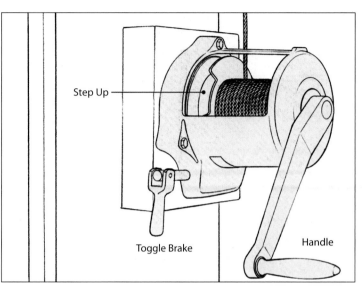

Step Up

Toggle Brake

Handle

On a reel winch, the entire line winds onto the reel, to which it remains attached permanently. The part of the drum next to the mast is stepped up to take the line's last two turns, which are kept in place by a notched metal flange. Otherwise, the tautened line might jam in the previous turns. Furthermore, if the line were left leading from the drum's outer edge, the tension might lever the winch off the mast. A brake locks the winch once the sail has been fully raised.

Easing a Sheet

To loosen a taut line gradually, keep tension on the tail with one hand while steadying the coils against the drum with the other. Avoid a rapid slip by easing the line out round the drum slowly and carefully—a thumb or finger can be crushed between line and winch.

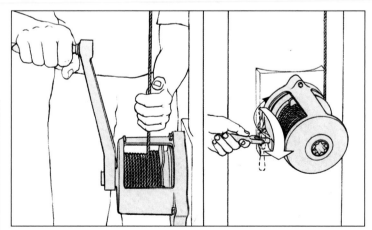

In raising a sail with a reel winch, as you crank distribute the wire evenly across the reel with your free hand *(left)* to preclude snarling. When the sail is up, remove the handle. The brake *(right)* should be on except when lowering sail. When lowering, back off the brake slightly to relieve tension on the halyard; then let the brake go completely to drop the sail. To operate the brake, raise the hinged toggle till it is at a right angle to the connecting shaft; then turn.

The crew lowers the mainsail in preparation for docking in the Adriatic Sea, Croatia.

Dockside Seamanship

Like all other aspects of sound seamanship, the success of docking is based on preparation and foresight. Dock lines and fenders must be readied, loose gear stowed away tidily and the decks cleared for action—all before the boat reaches the pier.

Whether the skipper approaches the dock in a sailboat or at the helm of a powerboat he should note carefully the positions of other vessels, and observe the direction of the wind and current. Whenever possible, the boat should approach against the wind or current; thus the skipper can figure out in advance which side of the boat will lie against the dock. He then orders his crew to begin rigging dock lines and fenders on the appropriate side.

One dock line should be belayed to the bow cleat, another to a stern cleat. Both are then led clear of all life lines and shrouds and brought back to be coiled on deck, ready for heaving ashore. Fenders, which contain

A fender board protects a boat from such dockside projections as pilings or cement abutments that often push aside a single fender and gouge topsides. The board, about four feet long, is buttressed by two fenders and suspended from the boat by a pair of lines set well apart to minimize swing.

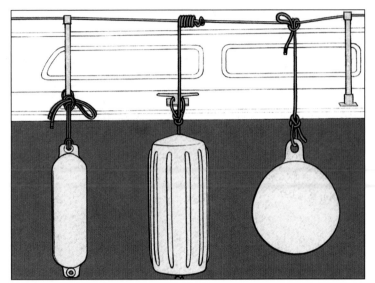

Fenders, which come in a variety of shapes and sizes, can be fastened to a boat in several ways. An air-filled plastic fender *(above, left)* is tied to a stanchion with two half hitches. A larger inflatable fender *(center)* is knotted to a cleat. And a slipped clove hitch supports a European circular fender from a life line.

a resilient substance such as cork or compressed air, are placed amidships where they keep the topsides from rubbing against the dock. They may be tied to life lines, stanchions or grab rails, or belayed to cleats *(above)*. Three fenders are usually sufficient insurance against chafed topsides. But if the boat is to lie against a piling, a fender board *(left)* will almost certainly be necessary.

Sometimes aboard a sizable sailboat, such as the 44-foot oceangoing sloop at left, the sails are lowered in advance, and the skipper then enters the dock area under auxiliary power. But in smaller vessels when winds are light and favorable, an experienced sailor may show off his skill by heading toward the dock under full sail. In either case, the sequence in lowering sails is the same: with the boat turned bow to the wind, the jib is normally struck first, then the mainsail. (Subsequently the jib should be folded and put into a sail bag and the mainsail either furled along the boom or bagged.)

As the boat comes into its berth, a crew member stationed up forward heaves the bow line to a dockside bystander—or steps nimbly ashore himself—and makes the line fast. The stern line is then run to the dock, spring lines are rigged and the fenders are adjusted. Then all the free lines are coiled and the craft made shipshape, as described on the following pages.

Tying Up at Docks

The dock lines that snug a boat into its berth may be arranged in a number of different ways depending on local conditions. But in each case the purpose of the dock lines is the same: to keep the boat close to its berth, while at the same time allowing enough play for the vessel to rise and fall with the tide, and to bob about naturally in the waves.

The system at right shows the basic lines that are used singly or in combination whenever a boat is made fast at a dock. In tying up, the bow line usually goes on first; then the stern line. Given the proper angle and amount of slack, these two will suffice for a brief stop. For more extended tie-ups, long diagonal lines called springs should be set to help steady the craft. Lines should never be cinched so hard that the boat and fenders are forced against the dock.

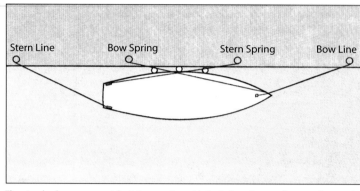

The standard arrangement for tying up alongside includes a bow and a stern line, each set at an angle of about 45° to hold the boat near the dock while still leaving room for the fenders—and some slack for the tide. The stern line may run to the offshore quarter, adding extra play to compensate for wind and tide. The bow and stern spring lines, set almost parallel to the boat, limit motion forward and back.

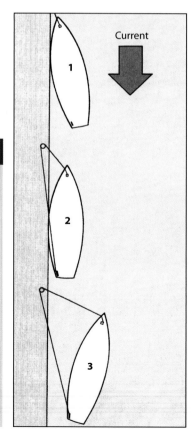

In areas of strong one-way current, two lines placed as indicated here will hold a boat in position. A crewman should fix a bow line about half a boat length forward at the bow (1), using a fender to keep the rail from hitting the dock. Then a spring line should be run from the stern, led well forward of the bow (2). As the current pushes on the vessel, tension on the spring line brings in the stern. Now the bow line should be slacked off slightly, letting the bow drift out until the keel rides against the current at an angle of about 5° (3)—far enough away from the dock to keep the hull from hitting it and chafing.

The Mediterranean Moor

Where dock space is limited, as in crowded Mediterranean ports, a boat may need to tie up stern to. First round up into the wind about 100 feet from the dock and drop the anchor. Back down toward the dock, paying out anchor line as you go, until you can step ashore and rig two spring lines from the stern. Then haul in enough anchor line to keep the stern clear of the dock. A pair of fenders keeps the stern from bumping the dock.

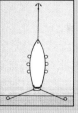

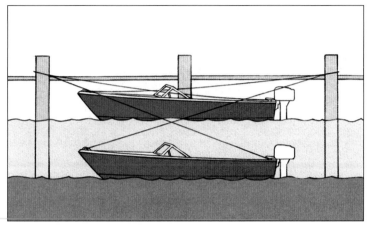

In waters with an extreme tidal range, extra-long spring lines should be set to allow a boat to rise and fall without drifting too far from the dock. If the lines are set at high tide, each one should be given a foot or two of slack. When the tide goes out, the vertical distance between the dock and the boat's deck—and thus the space the lines must span—will increase. But the increase will be slight compared with the entire length of each line, so that only a small amount of slack is needed. Bow and stern lines, if needed, should be extra long and angled well forward and aft, like the springs themselves.

When an incoming boat must tie up at a piling to which another line is already made fast, the arrangement shown here allows the first line to be cast off without disturbing the second one. The second eye should be run up through the eye of the original dock line and then dropped over the piling.

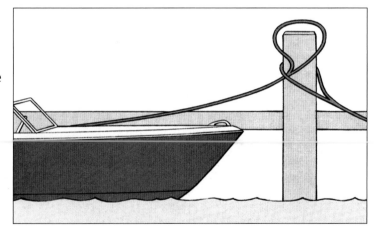

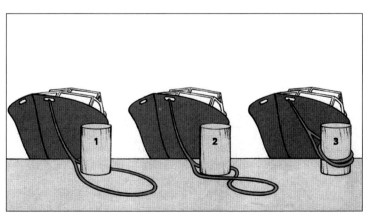

When a boat's bow and stern are significantly higher than the dock—or likely to become so because of a rise in the tide—the eyes of mooring lines should be double-looped to keep them from riding up over the piling and dropping off. In making fast, drop the eye over the piling (1). Twist the eye one half turn (2) and drop the loop thus formed back over the piling. This double loop will hold fast against an upward pull (3).

The Right and Easy Way

Stowing Ship

Before going ashore, a skipper and crew should take time to put their boat in order. Loose gear must be stowed, and fuel lines shut down. If the boat is to be empty for more than a few hours, the crew should close all seacocks and switch off the electrical system as well. Hatches must be closed—but air vents opened to prevent mustiness and to inhibit dry rot belowdecks. The decks are swabbed to remove grime, mud, and fuel spills, using water from a dockside hose or from buckets scooped from over the side *(below)*.

Made shipshape in this manner, a boat is not only more pleasant to come back to the next day, but considerably safer. A fuel line left open may allow gasoline fumes to seep into the cabin, creating a fire hazard. And boats have been known to fill up with water and sink, simply because the skipper forgot to close one of the seacocks.

To avert such disasters—and generally to keep their boats in order—many skippers carry a written check list like the one opposite, which is keyed to the cutaway drawing of a cabin cruiser. The list applies equally to sailboats, though sailors have a few more housekeeping chores *(pages 73–75)* before they can go ashore.

To Fetch a Pail of Water

When fetching up water with a bucket, do not just drop the bucket over the side—it tends to land face up and float rather than fill. To bring the bucket up full, first tie a line from the boat to the bucket handle. Holding the bucket upside down, throw it down hard at the water. As its lip catches the water, the bucket will capsize and fill. If the boat is underway, cast the bucket forward and haul it in before the line is straight up and down. Otherwise the bucket will run astern—possibly taking you with it.

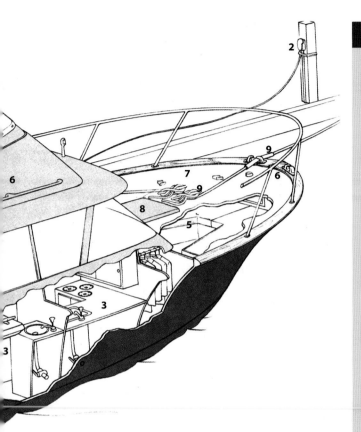

Powerboat Check List

1 Engine compartment: Close the fuel valves and any water inlet valves. Make sure that the air vents are clear.

2 Electrical system: Turn off the battery at its main cutoff switch. When using dockside power, be sure that the cord connection is secure and that it is watertight.

3 Galley and head: Turn off all faucets; close all seacocks; close the fuel line to the galley stove. Drain meltwater from the ice box; if leaving the boat for a long time, empty the ice box and leave its door ajar.

4 Bilge: Pump out the bilge and then shut the bilge-pump outlet valve.

5 Cabin: Stow loose gear. Close cabin drawers and lockers—unless the latter hold damp gear, in which case they should be left ajar. If any cabin cushions are damp, turn them on edge to air them. Secure the windows, portholes, and hatch covers.

6 Above decks: Wash dried salt from chrome and stainless-steel fittings with fresh water to prevent corrosion; dry with a chamois. Swab the decks. Dry woodwork with a sponge to forestall rot or varnish spotting.

7 Deck gear: Make sure all deck gear is lashed down or stowed away. Coil extra lines and stow them. Check that the anchor is chocked and lashed down, or stowed below.

8 Final lockup: Lock the lazarette and companionway door or hatch. If you have a canvas cover for the cockpit or flying bridge, snap it tightly in place.

9 Dock lines: As you disembark, check placement of dock lines and the tension on them; also check chafing gear and fenders.

The Right and Easy Way

The Right and Easy Way

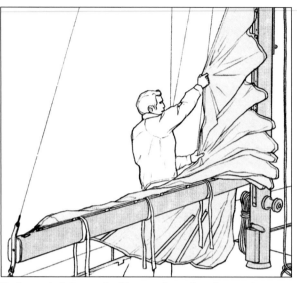

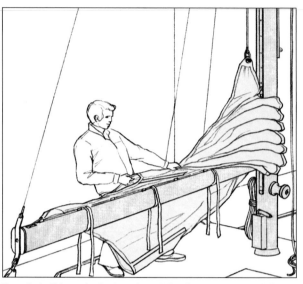

The first step in furling a mainsail is to wrap four or five sail stops—long strips of cloth—in round turns along the boom. Then, as the main is lowered, gather it on one side of the boom, pulling the bulk of sail aft as far as it will go; otherwise it will bunch near the mast. Fold the luff back and forth in pleats.

Next, slack off the outhaul to keep the sail's foot from stretching while furled. Now, starting near the mast, pull on the sail's leech and work the bulk of the sail aft toward the clew; bundle the cloth into loose folds as you go. Battens should be laid parallel to the boom—or removed from the sail and stowed.

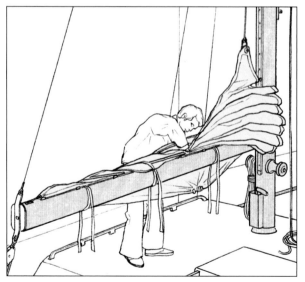

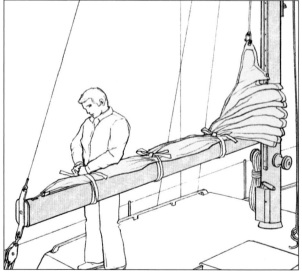

The third step is to form the sail into a tight bundle along the top of the boom. Working aft from the mast, grasp the sail near its foot, creating a hammock of cloth into which the rest of the sail can then be stuffed. Shake the folds of sailcloth into this hammock and roll it onto the top of the boom.

As each portion of sail is rolled onto the top of the boom, tie the bundle of furled sail in place with sail stops. Bring the ends of each sail stop up over the furl and secure them with a slipped reef knot; if the reef knot is not slipped, it is likely to jam, since sail stops are of such bulky material.

Buttoning Up a Sailboat

Putting a sailboat to bed requires the same systematic procedures used on a powerboat—but with a few additional steps for securing the sails, rigging and the relatively more complex deck gear. Headsails should be put into sail bags and then stowed belowdecks. Mainsails may be either furled along the boom *(left)* or, on small boats, removed and bagged.

A bit of extra care in furling and bagging the sails helps preserve their working life and their appearance. Since moisture breeds mildew, sails should be thoroughly dried before long-term stowing. If the wind is light, they can be hoisted partway to flap gently in the breeze; otherwise, dry them ashore on the ground.

When the mainsail is furled, a fitted sail cover *(right)* guards it from weathering and also keeps off the sun, which deteriorates its synthetic fibers. In stowing other sails, fold them neatly to minimize creases; simply stuffing a sail into its bag may cause sharp creases that will interfere with smooth airflow along its surface.

Once the sails have been bagged or furled, secure the boat's boom and helm, coil its lines and otherwise make it shipshape, as shown on the following pages.

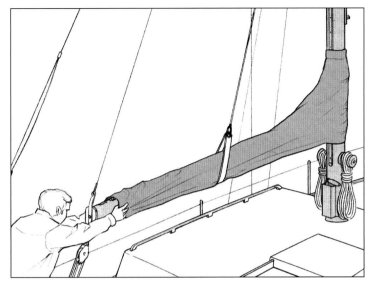

To put on a mainsail cover, start at the forward end and lace the collar of the sail cover tightly around the mast, inside the halyards. Bring the rest of the cover aft over the furled sail, lacing it under the boom as you go; secure it at the end of the boom with the tail end of the line used for lacing. The main halyard is then led away from the mast, as shown here, and shackled to the boom vang strap, which is looped upside down around the middle of the boom.

To fold a headsail, first lay it out flat in an open area such as the foredeck or on a dock. Then imagine a set of fold lines, shown here as broken lines (1), running parallel to the luff and spaced slightly closer than the diameter of the sail bag. Fold the sail back and forth, as illustrated, until it forms a narrow strip (2). Roll the sail loosely from the foot (3), leaving the hanks, head, tack and clew exposed for easy access next time out, and slip it into the bag (4).

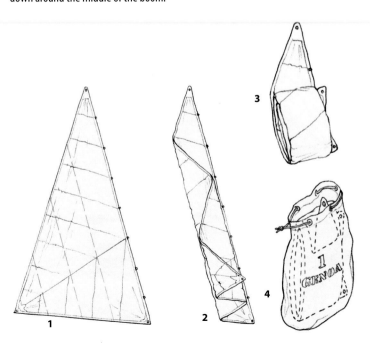

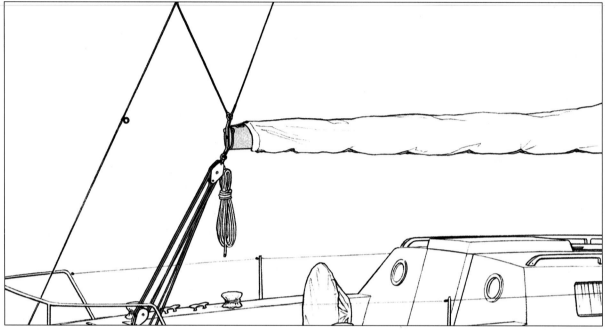

In securing a sailboat, after the sails have been furled tie the boom firmly amidships, using the arrangement of three lines shown here. The topping lift, running from the masthead, supports the boom's weight. The mainsheet, pulled in and cleated, keeps the boom from bouncing up or swinging back and forth. The third line, run from the backstay, also inhibits swing and provides support; it is unnecessary if the boom rests in a support called a boom crotch *(opposite)*.

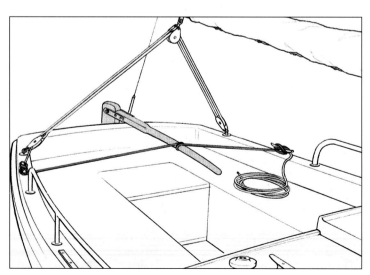

A line running athwartships and wrapped around a boat's tiller prevents the tiller and rudder from slatting back and forth with the motion of the boat. Here, the mainsheet, pulled in hard and cleated to starboard, loops around the tiller and then runs to a cleat on the port side. Some skippers, preferring to hang the mainsheet in a coil from the boom *(top)*, secure the tiller with a separate line. Or they may wedge the tiller between parts of the mainsheet tackle *(opposite)*.

Sailboat Check List

1 Sails: Furl and cover the mainsail, or stow it in a sail bag. Bag all headsails and stow them.

2 Spars and helm: Secure the boom and helm, using any of the methods on these pages. Unship and stow the rudder if it is removable. Also, raise the centerboard if you have one.

3 Wire rigging: Attach the shackle ends of all halyards to convenient fittings. Run the jib and spinnaker halyards forward to a foredeck fitting or to the bow pulpit. Lead the main halyard to the boom vang strap on the boom.

4 Rope rigging: Cleat and coil halyard tails and permanent sheets. Hang coils off the deck to dry. Unreeve, coil and stow other lines.

5 Halyard ties: Using lengths of line or shock cord led from the shrouds, tie standing parts of halyards so they will not slat on the mast.

6 Deck hardware: Stow all portable deck hardware. Check jib-sheet tracks to make sure the snatch blocks have been stowed. Be sure all winch handles have been stowed.

7 Protective coverings: When leaving the boat for several days or more, cover the winches, and also the wheel and binnacle, if any.

8 Heavy gear: Lash down the spinnaker pole. Lash the anchor into its chocks on deck, or else unshackle it and stow it below.

9 Final lockup: Close down any fuel lines, seacocks and the electric system. Pump the bilge; check air vents; secure hatches; swab the decks. And as you leave, be sure mooring lines, chafing gear and fenders are secure.

CHAPTER 3:

Dropping Anchor

An anchor is a universal symbol of security and steadfastness. To fulfill its promise, however, an anchor must be properly matched to a given boat and to the types of bottoms it will encounter. The anchor's complementary rigging, especially the anchor line, or rode, must be selected with these factors in mind and with some anticipation of the water depths in which it will probably be used. And the boatman must know how to pick his spot to drop the anchor in. Otherwise all that potential security can, literally, be lost, as one hapless party of fishermen learned when they attempted to moor their small outboard on a calm day off the New Jersey coast. Instead of a proper anchor, they had a bucket filled with concrete attached to a mere 20 feet of line. And instead of lowering the rig gently, they simply heaved it overboard—into 40 feet of water. When the bucket hit the end of the line, its weight yanked out the cleat to which the other end of the rode was fastened, tearing a large hole in the aluminum hull.

In trying to moor their craft with a shapeless mass of dead weight, these fishermen were a kind of throwback to prehistoric boatmen, whose anchors were heavy stones tied to lengths of braided fibers and dropped overboard—perhaps with occasional similar consequences. The first known anchors designed to hold by virtue of their shapes rather than sheer mass were developed about 2000 B.C. by East India seafarers, who fashioned king-sized fishhooks, each with a single prong. By 600 B.C. the Greeks had added another prong, or fluke, plus a crosspiece at the top to help position the flukes for grabbing the bottom. Eventually, specialized anchors such as those shown on the following pages evolved from the classic shape *(page 78)*, so that a mariner could safely moor on any kind of bottom.

Today's sailor should take the time and care to find out about these different kinds of anchors and their capabilities and shortcomings. He should know how long and how strong a rope to use. In selecting an anchorage he should consult charts of the area and seek local advice to find a snug anchorage. And when he has picked his spot, he must lower the hook with care. The sagacious skipper will, in addition, carry at least one extra anchor; some boats are equipped with as many as four, of different designs and weights, for insurance against a lost anchor and for coping with varying bottoms and weather.

This lightweight Danforth anchor is properly stowed before use. It is especially effective in sand and mud.

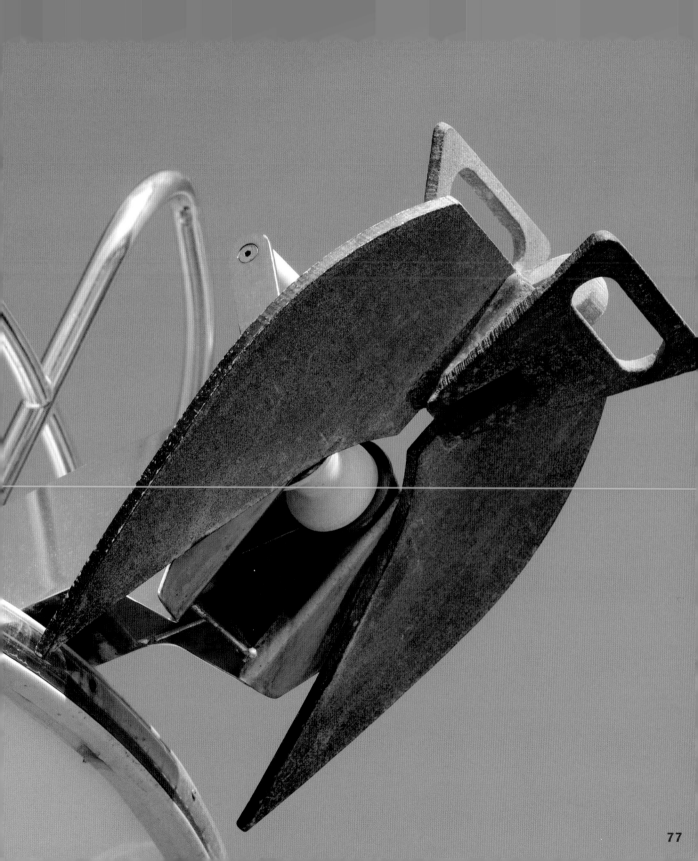

The Common Anchors

Although anchors come in a variety of shapes, weights, and capabilities, most of them share a number of common structural elements. Every anchor but the mushroom *(below)* has one or more flukes that grab onto the bottom; and all have a shank that joins the holding component at the crown and a ring or a hole for attaching the anchor line, or rode. Many anchors also incorporate a crosspiece called a stock, which helps position them properly so that the flukes can sink home.

In choosing an anchor, a boat handler should select a design and weight compatible with his vessel *(chart, page 91)*. And he should learn which kinds of hooks hold best in sand, mud, seaweed, gravel, rock, loose shells, etc. Stowing and ease of handling are important considerations, too: folding anchors tuck away as neatly as a furled umbrella, for instance; and no small-craft anchor should be too heavy to drop or retrieve easily by hand.

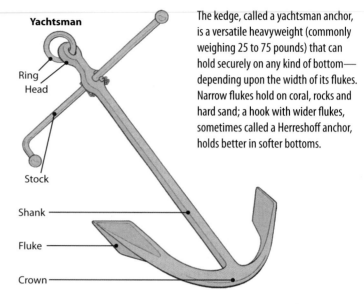

Yachtsman

Ring
Head

Stock

Shank

Fluke

Crown

The kedge, called a yachtsman anchor, is a versatile heavyweight (commonly weighing 25 to 75 pounds) that can hold securely on any kind of bottom—depending upon the width of its flukes. Narrow flukes hold on coral, rocks and hard sand; a hook with wider flukes, sometimes called a Herreshoff anchor, holds better in softer bottoms.

Plow

The middleweight plow anchor buries itself readily in soft mud, and is also effective in penetrating weeds and shell beds. Moreover, a hinge on the shank helps the plow to remain buried when the angle of pull on the rode changes with shifts in wind or current.

The Durable Mushroom

As a permanent mooring, a heavy mushroom (100 to 500 pounds) makes the best anchor. It settles deeply into soft bottoms, has no projecting stock or flukes to foul, and the moored vessel can swing freely around the anchor without dislodging it.

Danforth

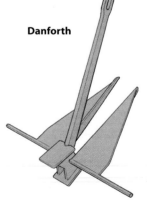

The lightweight (two and a half pounds and up) Danforth is excellent for small- and medium-sized boats. Especially effective in sand or mud, the broad-based flukes respond to horizontal pull on the hinged shank by digging down, often burying the whole hook. The stock, at the crown end, is in the same plane as the flukes, so the anchor stows flat.

The lightweight Northill anchor, once standard equipment for tethering seaplanes has a stock at the crown end that slides out and folds up against the shank for stowing. In use, when one of the sharp flukes sinks into soft mud, the stock will dig in and take hold as well, reinforcing the anchor's grip.

Northill

The flukes of a folding anchor (here shown in the open position) can be snugged up against its shank, secured with a ring and stowed in a minimum of space. Reopened and tossed overboard, the folding anchor, like the grapnel, is most effective when it hooks rock or coral. Many boatmen take these convenient folding anchors for spares, and some racing sailors conform to class-boat rules by carrying lightweight models.

Folding

Dropping Anchor

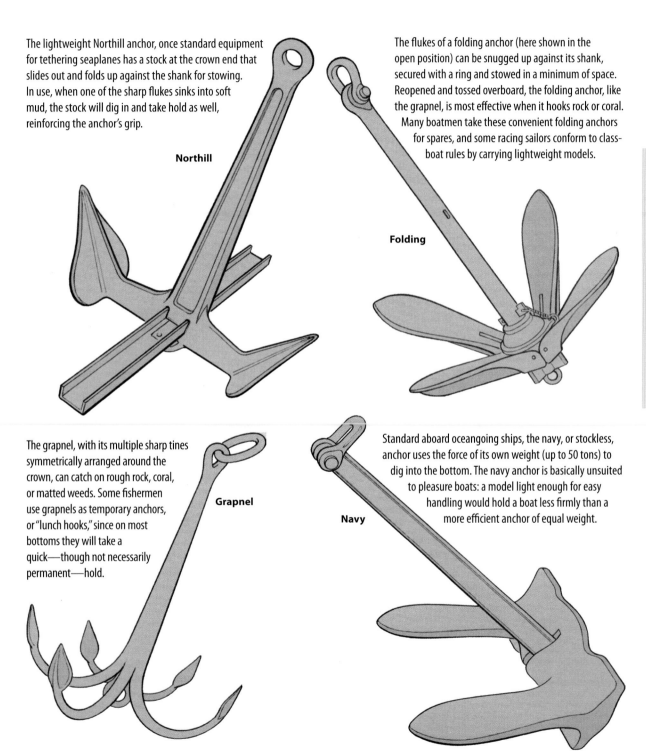

The grapnel, with its multiple sharp tines symmetrically arranged around the crown, can catch on rough rock, coral, or matted weeds. Some fishermen use grapnels as temporary anchors, or "lunch hooks," since on most bottoms they will take a quick—though not necessarily permanent—hold.

Grapnel

Standard aboard oceangoing ships, the navy, or stockless, anchor uses the force of its own weight (up to 50 tons) to dig into the bottom. The navy anchor is basically unsuited to pleasure boats: a model light enough for easy handling would hold a boat less firmly than a more efficient anchor of equal weight.

Navy

How Anchors Hold

All anchors are designed to get a grip as quickly as possible after they hit bottom. They take hold in one of two basic ways. Some of them hook into the ground—or onto a rock or coral outcropping—with one of their sharp flukes. Others, designed especially for soft bottoms, bury themselves, flukes, shank, and all.

Neither a hooking anchor nor a burying type will start holding, however, until enough rode has been payed out so that the angle of pull allows the tips of the flukes to bite. Seamen speak of this angle of pull in terms of scope, which is roughly defined as the relationship between the depth of the water and the length of the rode. In practice, water depth should be figured as the distance from a boat's bow chock to the bottom: when a boat with three feet of freeboard is in nine feet of water, the anchoring depth is 12 feet.

As shown in the drawings at right, the greater the scope, the more efficient is the angle of pull on the anchor. A length of chain attached to the rode's lower end not only resists chafe against rocks and gravel, but helps weigh the rode down and flatten its angle. Burying anchors work best with a scope of about 7 to 1 (a rode seven times as long as the distance from bow to bottom); hooking anchors require less scope under normal conditions, but must be heavier than a burying anchor to provide an equivalent holding power. When a boat is riding out a storm, both types should be given a scope of about 10 to 1. In any weather, the skipper should calculate his scope for the water depth at high tide; otherwise a boat anchored at low tide may uproot its anchor when the rising water changes the angle of pull.

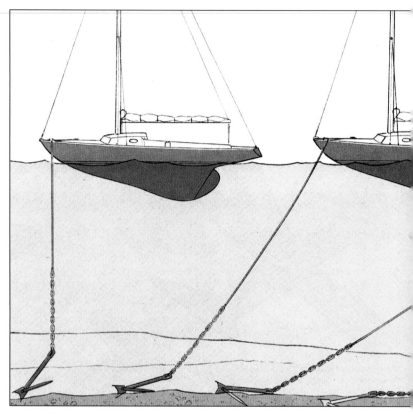

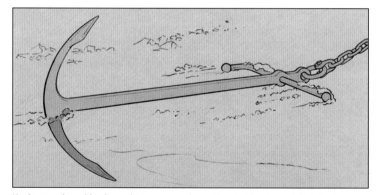

Hooking anchors, like the yachtsman type above, thrust at least one fluke into the bottom, much as a pickax penetrates the earth. The fluke falls into position to dig in because the stock, set at right angles to it, tends to lie flat on the bottom. Then the horizontal pull resulting from a combination of heavy chain and generous scope permits the strain on the rode to drive in the fluke.

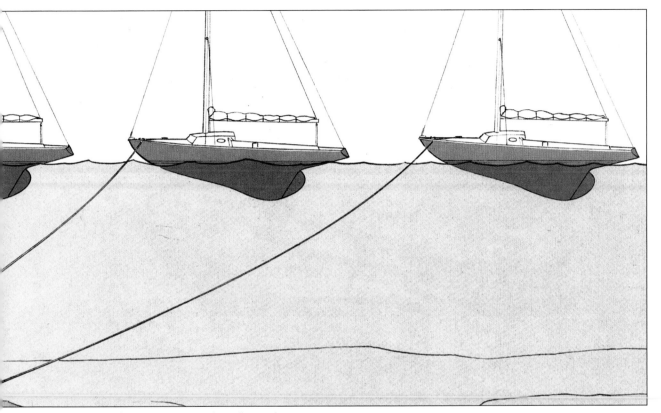

The importance of scope in setting an anchor is illustrated above. A burying anchor of the popular Danforth type is lowered straight down. While the rode is still vertical, the scope is 1 to 1 and the anchor is ineffectual. As more rode is payed out, the anchor falls so that the flukes lie flat and then begin to dig in. Finally, as in the right-hand sketch, the flukes bury themselves entirely.

Burying anchors, like the plow type above or the Danforth at top, often dig themselves entirely underground in a muddy or a loose, sandy bottom. An initial tug on the plow's shank sets the anchor's single fluke into position to burrow in. After it is firmly set, the hinged shank lets the boat swing around the anchor without disengaging it.

Dropping Anchor

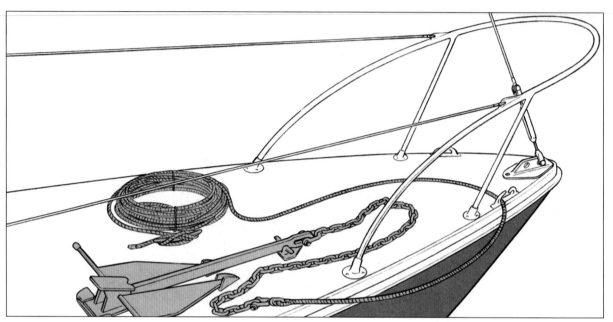

Though still secured to the deck with fittings called anchor chocks, the Danforth hook shown above is rigged and ready for letting go. The rode's bitter end, off the bottom of the coil, is made fast to the mooring cleat, and the line is coiled neatly and secured with marline. The other end has been passed through the bow chocks and back around the pulpit so the anchor can be easily put overboard. When freed from its lashings, the rode will feed smoothly from the top as the anchor goes down.

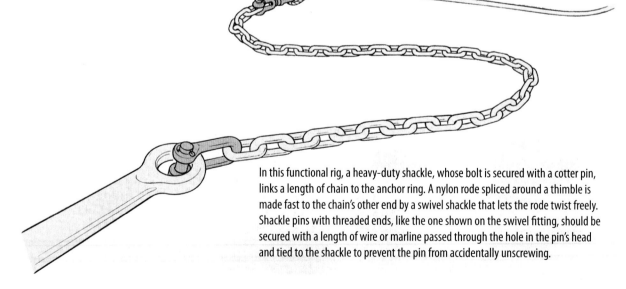

In this functional rig, a heavy-duty shackle, whose bolt is secured with a cotter pin, links a length of chain to the anchor ring. A nylon rode spliced around a thimble is made fast to the chain's other end by a swivel shackle that lets the rode twist freely. Shackle pins with threaded ends, like the one shown on the swivel fitting, should be secured with a length of wire or marline passed through the hole in the pin's head and tied to the shackle to prevent the pin from accidentally unscrewing.

When ready to drop the hook, a sailboat skipper should approach his selected spot from downwind, as though he were picking up a mooring. The crew, meanwhile, lowers the jib (1) so the flapping sail will not interfere with his work. As the boat rounds up into the wind, the crew makes sure the rode will run free, and that its bitter end is secured. He waits until the boat loses way and begins drifting backward before he lowers the anchor overboard (2) and pays out the rode hand over hand (3) to its proper scope. He next snubs the rode (4) to set the anchor firmly, and then cleats the line.

When anchoring under power, the engine can be used to set the anchor and test its grip on the bottom. Like the sailboat skipper, the power man approaches from downwind, coming to a dead stop over the spot where the anchor is to be dropped. As the anchor hits bottom, the helmsman goes into slow reverse. When the proper scope has been let out, the rode is snubbed, and the pull of the engine will drive the anchor home. A burst of moderate throttle will then ensure that the anchor is firmly set and will not drag.

The Anchor Watch

After the boatman has dropped anchor, he should take a few precautions to make sure the anchor is firmly set. Markers along the rode *(below, right)* tell him how deep the water is and how much line he has payed out. Calculating his desired scope, he lets off as much extra rode as the situation demands, then cleats the rode securely. Where the rode passes through the bow chocks, he makes sure it is protected from chafing *(right)*.

For the next half hour or so, someone should stay aboard the boat, checking its position in relation to boats anchored nearby and to objects on shore, as shown opposite. If the boat stays in a relatively fixed position, the anchor is probably holding firmly. But an anchor can start to drag for any number of reasons. It may, for example, not have dug in properly; the bottom may be rocky; or the anchor may have fouled its rode because it was thrown carelessly overboard or because the rode went out in a tangle.

Even the well-embedded anchor may sometimes break out and drag in a sudden strong wind—or if a shift of wind or current abruptly alters the direction of pull on the anchor. Normally the anchor will reset itself, but sometimes bottom debris has so fouled the flukes that the anchor cannot dig in. In this latter case, the anchor should be raised, cleaned off, and again lowered to the bottom.

The crewman above is fixing a rode so it will not chafe in a bow chock. In choppy waters that rock the boat constantly, burrs on a bow chock can cut through a rode in a few hours. Chafing gear can be improvised from rags or canvas; but a tougher, more permanent device is shown here—a piece of neoprene hose split lengthwise and tied at each end to the anchor rode with marline.

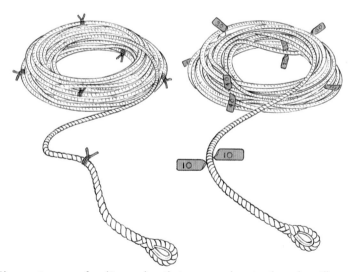

Above are two ways of marking a rode so that a crewman lowering the anchor will know how much line he has let out. The numbered plastic tags on the far coil are easy to affix, but also tear off easily, and are hard to read at night. The more durable markings on the other coil can be read by touch. Pieces of marline or leather are tied around a rode and coded by knots—one knot for the first 20 feet (or other unit of measure), two for the next, then three; then back to one, two and three for the next units, and so on.

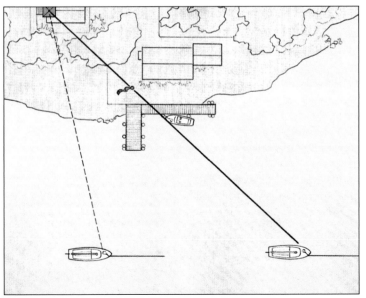

To check for anchor drag, a crewman lines up shoreline landmarks that are neither directly astern nor dead ahead of the boat—here, a flagpole and a church spire. Then he reads the boat's heading from the compass. For the next half hour or so he frequently rechecks the boat's heading and sights the landmarks. Small changes in alignment, along with changes in heading, usually mean only that wind or current has turned the boat slightly or moved it around the anchor. But if the compass heading stays unchanged and the landmarks shift widely out of line as shown at left, then the anchor is dragging.

Getting a Firmer Hold

In most situations a boat's everyday working anchor provides plenty of holding power, particularly if the boatman has taken care to equip his craft with the proper anchor *(chart, opposite at bottom)*. But certain conditions—such as strong winds, swift currents, or steep waves—demand more holding power. For these infrequent but inevitable situations, a good seaman is prepared in a number of ways.

First, he carries aboard a storm anchor—at least 60 percent heavier than the working anchor—that he uses when he expects winds of about 30 knots or more. The storm anchor usually has its own, stronger rode permanently attached to it. The big hook should provide double the holding power of the working anchor.

Sometimes, though, the storm anchor's effectiveness is reduced by the action of waves that toss the boat around. The lunging vessel jerks heavily on the rode, putting a harsh strain on the bow cleat and threatening to break the hook loose from the bottom. Two antidotes for this circumstance are illustrated in the drawings at right. Both reduce the chance of the anchor's breaking out by preventing the rode from coming up taut—as does the ingenious shock absorber *(right)* used for an all-chain rode.

Finally, there are times when even the best laid single anchor will not do the job; then a second anchor must be put overboard, as described on pages 92–93.

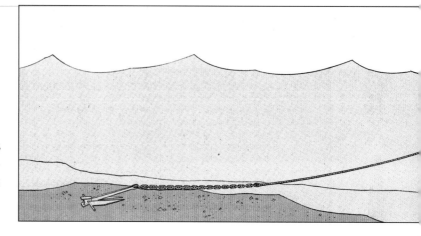

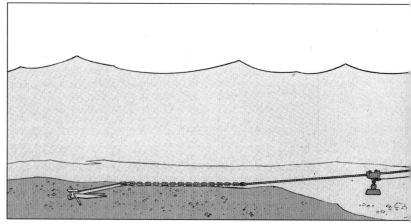

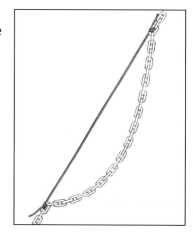

A length of stretchy nylon secured across a slightly longer length of chain—about five feet of nylon to six feet of chain—makes an all-chain anchor rode more shock absorbent. Whenever waves pitch the boat up and down, jerking on the rode, the nylon takes the initial strain and stretches, gentling the jolts on both the anchor and the boat's fittings.

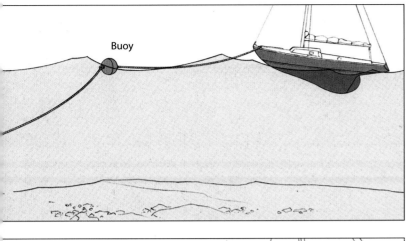

Buoy

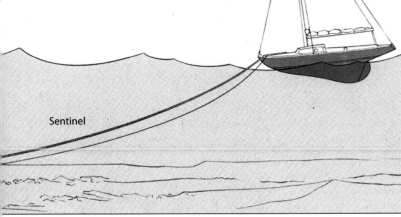

Sentinel

The two illustrations at left show how to increase an anchor's holding power by providing a counterpull at a different angle from the direction of the main strain on the rode. In the top drawing, the rode is held up with a plastic mooring buoy pierced by a steel rod with a ring at each end. The rode is attached to one end of the rod and the boat is attached to the other by a boat length of line of the same diameter as the rode. The lower drawing shows a sentinel (also called a kellet), which is simply a mass of dead weight—anything from a spare anchor to a pig of lead will do. The sentinel is usually attached to the rode by a special fitting called a saddle (shown in the drawing) and lowered two thirds of the way down the rode by a light line. Either of these rigs—a typical 12-inch buoy or a 30-pound sentinel—if used with a 7 to 1 scope, cushions any jerking action so effectively that twice the normal force is required to jerk the rode taut.

Dropping Anchor

Suiting the Anchor to the Boat

Length of Boat	Danforth Hi-Tensile	Danforth Standard	Plow	Northill	Yachtsman
15 feet	5 lbs.	4 lbs.	10 lbs.	6 lbs.	20 lbs.
20	5	8	15	12	25
25	5	8	15	12	35
30	12	13	20	27	35
35	12	22	25	27	45
40	20	22	35	46	65
45	20	40	45	46	75
50	20	40	45	46	100
55	35	65	60	80	125

The chart at left offers a guide to the proper weight of working anchors for vessels of various lengths. Five of the most popular kinds of anchors are listed here; the Hi-Tensile Danforth differs from the standard model in being somewhat more efficient and stronger per pound—and more expensive. Since boats of equal size but differing designs can behave quite differently at anchor, a skipper should consult owners of craft similar to his own when he buys his ground tackle.

Doubling Up for Safety

Two anchors—one a storm anchor, the other the vessel's regular hook—set ahead of the boat with their rodes at no more than a 45° angle can provide substantially more holding power than a single hook. They will also reduce the boat's freedom to swing. To set the second anchor, a powerboatman can motor up abreast of his first anchor, drop the other, then let the boat fall back until the rodes are of equal length. A sailboat skipper, by slacking the first anchor's rode, can sail into position to drop the other; but if a dinghy is handy and the water calm, he may find it simpler to row out the second anchor.

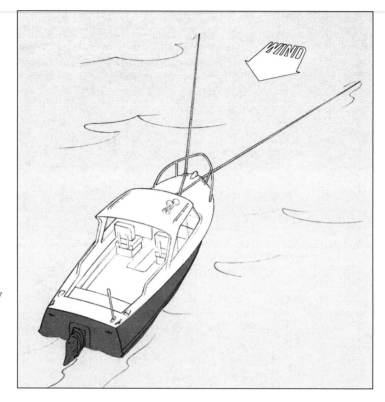

A second anchor put out astern lets a boat anchor near a fixed obstacle, such as a buoy or a sandbar, by limiting sideways movement to as little as three or four boat widths. The skipper sets the bow anchor first, then goes into reverse or falls downwind or downcurrent until he has payed out twice his normal scope. He lowers the stern anchor, then hauls in the bow rode until the boat is midway between the anchors. Such bow and stern anchoring should be avoided if either wind or current is likely to shift abeam; the push against the tethered boat's side could break loose one or both anchors.

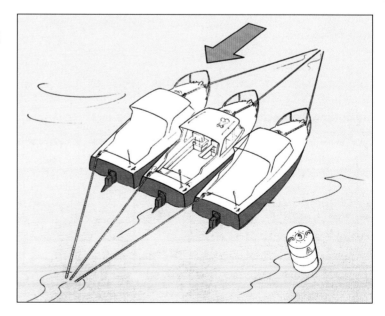

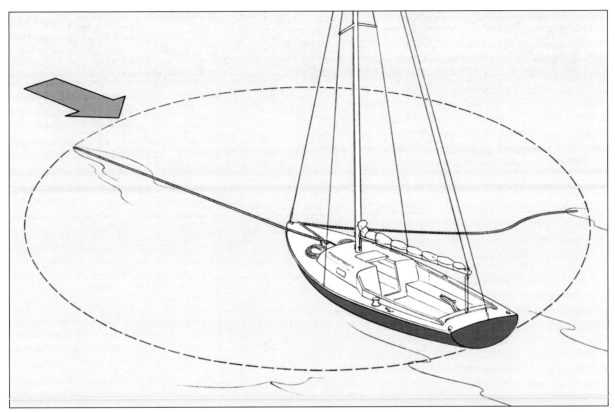

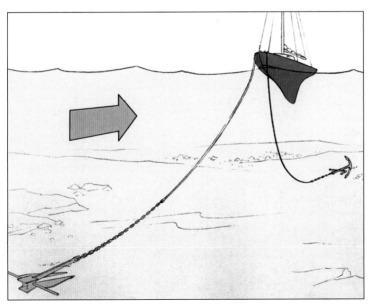

In areas of strong tides, two anchors set from the bow, well apart and in line with the current, add security and limit the boat's swing to a circle of about two boat lengths in diameter. In this so-called Bahamian moor—named for its frequent use in the strong currents of those islands' narrow channels—the first anchor is put overboard upcurrent from where the boat will lie. Then the boatman lets his craft drift backward until he has let off twice the normal scope—and drops the second anchor, also from the bow. Finally, he pulls in on the first rode until he is an equal distance from the two anchors.

Weighing Anchor

Weighing anchor is normally a smooth, relatively quick and simple procedure. The skipper first starts his engine or hoists his mainsail, to be ready to go as the anchor breaks loose. When the boat reaches a point just above the anchor, normally it can be pulled free with a quick tug; whereupon the crew hauls it up, washes off any mud and brings it aboard.

But sometimes the anchor will get stuck, usually because a fluke has become wedged in a crevice or has buried itself deeply in heavy mud. A skipper cannot prevent such a mishap, but he can prepare his anchor beforehand, as shown at right, so that a snagged fluke can be quickly dislodged from the bottom.

If, however, the anchor has not been prerigged, the boatman may try hauling in the rode and cleating it just as it becomes vertical. The boat's forward momentum on the shortened rode may free the anchor. Similarly, in a swell, the crew can snub the rode hard when the bow drops into a wave trough; as the bow lifts again, it may pull up the anchor. Finally, the boatman can try sailing or powering around the anchor with the rode taut, as shown below, until he finds the angle of pull that will jerk the anchor loose. Once free, he waits until the crew has the anchor aboard and secured in its chocks before setting off at cruising speed for the next destination.

A powerboat skipper who tries to pull a jammed anchor free by circling it should be sure the rode is cleated down hard and the tension on it maintained. A sailboat skipper can sometimes dislodge a snagged anchor by first letting out enough rode to provide room for maneuvering and then tacking back and forth over the anchor until he finds an angle at which it will pull free.

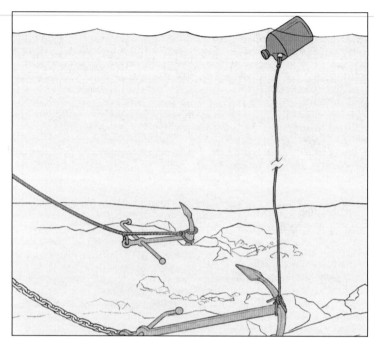

In one method of prerigging an anchor, a so-called tripping line is tied to the anchor's crown and buoyed to the surface. If a fluke becomes jammed, a vertical tug on the line will lift the anchor straight out. In another prerigging method called scowing, the rode is first tied securely to the anchor's crown, then lashed lightly to the head with marline. When weighing anchor, the rode is shortened until it is vertical; then a sharp tug on the rode breaks the marline and up comes the anchor, crown first. A scowed anchor is handy for brief stops, but it may break loose prematurely if the boat swings.

As a crewman hauls in the rode, the boat rides up toward its anchor. When the rode is vertical and the boat directly above the anchor, a tug on the line should break the hook loose. When the anchor is clear of the bottom, the crew signals the skipper and then lifts the anchor aboard, taking care not to gouge the topsides. Although a sailboat usually stays pointed with its head to wind throughout this procedure so that the hoisted mainsail luffs, a powerboat skipper can ease the crewman's job by motoring the craft slowly up to the anchor.

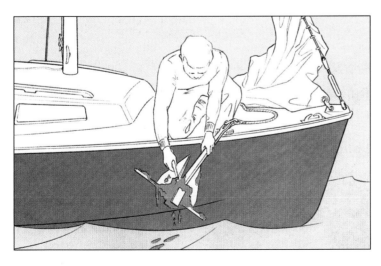

Bottom mud clinging to the flukes must be cleaned off before an anchor is brought aboard—otherwise it can begrime topsides, deck, and bilge. A swab or a brush may be necessary to scour away clay or dense mud, as here. An anchor covered with loose mud, however, will clean itself if allowed to drag through the water just below the surface as the boat moves slowly ahead.

CHAPTER 4:
Dealing with Foul Weather

Stormy weather is a part of every boatman's life. Though he may never have to deal with the 40-knot-and-over gales encountered by the ocean racers *(pages 112–115),* occasional encounters with dirty weather are inevitable. Summer squalls can kick up in a matter of minutes. And even on a clear day, steady winds of 15 knots and up, sweeping over a stretch of open water, can build up wave action that is difficult or downright dangerous for the boatman who is unprepared to deal with it.

Under such conditions, modern boats are designed to withstand extraordinary physical punishment. But they can be terribly vulnerable to bad judgment or to the eroded capacity of a sick or tired crew.

A close watch on the weather and careful attention to forecasts before sailing are advisable. Heavy-weather tactics such as reefing *(pages 106–107)* should be practiced in fair weather. If a healthy breeze or heavy clouds are building offshore, foul weather gear should be put on at the dock or at least stowed close at hand. For even the most skilled seaman is less effective after he has been cold and wet for awhile. Care must be taken that the lines attached to safety harnesses are long enough to allow room for crewmen to move during such tasks as taking down a headsail. Forethought must be given to emergency gear.

As important as any aspect of heavy-weather preparation—and often neglected by novices—is the unglamorous business of coping with seasickness. Although some people are more susceptible to *mal de mer* than others, no one is totally immune, and no one should be embarrassed to admit susceptibility. Some cases can be cured simply by lying down—but a stricken sailor on his back is unable to help the ship, and all hands would be far better off if he had taken motion-sickness pills beforehand. In fact, all hands would do well to eat heartily, sleep long and drink no more than moderately before venturing onto the open water. For alcohol, fatigue and an empty stomach can all help to induce queasiness.

However, a healthy crew on a well-prepared boat need experience no anxiety or real trouble when a storm hits. Instead they can concentrate on their primary foul-weather mission: attempting to achieve a harmony between boat and sea. With powerboats, this is achieved primarily with wheel and throttle. Sailboat crews have the more complex task of progressively reducing sail, by reefing and changing headsails, as the wind increases. Eventually, if a storm becomes so violent that continuing the voyage may be impossible or unsafe, then the boatman must know how to heave to and ride out the gale.

A crewman clad in foul weather gear steers a sailboat into rough weather.

The well-equipped sailor above is wearing a lightweight waterproof pullover parka with wrist snaps and a drawstring hood. His waterproof trousers are secured with ankle straps. As insurance against falling overboard, he wears a safety harness consisting of a belt and suspender-like straps, which prevent the belt from being pulled off him in the event of a tumble. A stout line attached to the belt ends with a clip, which is made fast to a life line. A pair of sneakers with nonskid soles provide traction on a wet deck.

Hot food helps to keep sailors strong and happy. Formerly, the galley of a storm-tossed boat might have been a scrambled madhouse, but modern design concepts have solved some of the problems. The sea cook at right is wearing foul weather pants as protection against splashes of hot liquids. The stove is slung on gimbals to keep it level. Hooked to the cook's galley belt are three stays. One, attached to the boat's side, holds him when the vessel heels; the others, led fore and aft, help him when the craft pitches.

Foul Weather Gear

Suitable foul weather clothing is an essential part of a boatman's gear, and the farther offshore he plans to venture, the more sturdily it should be made. Boats have sunk in storms because their poorly clad crews were too cold and wet and tired to perform their duties.

A proper seagoing wardrobe includes waterproof pants and hooded jacket, preferably finished in gaudy colors that can be easily spotted should a crewman go overboard. These garments should be loose-fitting to go over sweaters and sneakers, and they should be easy to put on quickly in an emergency.

Moreover, these clothes should be put on sooner rather than later. For, as any experienced boatman can attest, if he gets wet before he can don foul weather gear, it is virtually impossible for him to dry out until the crisis has passed and he can change clothes. Cold, too, tends to persist. Good foul weather clothes not only keep water out but keep body heat in.

Styles in such gear have changed in recent years. The traditional fisherman's slicker, or oilskins, gave way to rubberized rainwear, which in turn has been succeeded by tough, waterproof plastics. For the deep-water sailor, the heavy rubberized clothing is best—despite the fact that it can be uncomfortably sweaty. In warm climates, a yachtsman may prefer light-weight plastic-coated nylon fabrics.

The sailor above wears heavy rubberized bib overalls, with ankle bands to prevent water from sloshing into his high rubber sea boots, which also have nonskid soles. The bright orange jacket will make him visible if he falls overboard. His hat has a wide back brim to keep water from running down his neck. Many sailors also wrap towels around their necks to absorb trickling water.

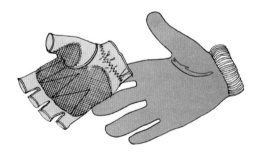

The larger of the two seagoing gloves above has been waterproofed with sprayed-on neoprene to keep hands dry and snug—though at the expense of manual dexterity. These full-fingered gloves are very useful for helmsmen, whose hands are exposed for long stretches at the tiller or wheel. The fingerless glove, handy for tying knots or handling lines, has a reinforced palm to provide extra grip and protection when handling wet lines, but it exposes the fingers to the elements.

Handling Head Seas

Maneuvering through heavy seas under either sail or power calls for skilled and steady helmsmanship, as shown in the photographs on these and the following pages. Rough water is particularly troublesome for the fast, planing-type powerboats, whose designers have achieved speed and maneuverability at some cost in seaworthiness.

Such craft are speedy enough to outrun really dangerous heavy weather if the skipper has kept up with the latest forecasts. But unpredictable caprices of nature, such as thunderstorms, can build up in minutes and surprise the wariest skipper of the fastest powerboat.

When rough seas are unavoidable, the first rule for negotiating them is to adjust the speed of the boat so that the hull can move more in harmony with waves.

The best rough-water pace for most high-powered boats is just below the speed at which the boat begins to plane. This keeps the hull deep enough in the water so that the rudder and the propeller do not lose effectiveness, while the bow lifts enough to prevent its burying. Even when the helmsman finds the right speed, he should keep a hand on the throttle ready to adjust the speed of his boat to accommodate any approaching comber.

A common mistake of fledgling skippers is speeding into head seas. The powerboat crashing into the waves above has nosed into the air, limiting the skipper's control and field of vision, and setting up the hull for a jarring comedown in a trough.

Crashing into the trough of a wave, the fast-moving speedboat drenches its deck with spray and badly jars its occupant. Such a jolt strains the boat's fixtures and, if the craft is overloaded or badly trimmed, could seriously damage the vessel or injure those aboard.

The skipper of this powerboat properly slows his craft so that it travels comfortably. Moving at about 15 miles per hour, the boat rides over a wave's crest, maintaining sufficient contact with the water to counteract the wind's tendency to blow the boat sideways and out of control.

Still firmly in control, the powerboat slides easily into the trough of the wave, slicing the sea with its bow instead of pounding down upon its broader midships sections.

No water sloshes over the deck or into the cockpit. The driver has not been jarred, and he has a clear view across the bow to the next wave.

Running before the Sea

Running before heavy seas is usually more comfortable than slogging into them. But it can also be more dangerous. Sometimes a powerboatman is able to adjust his speed to ride for long stretches just behind the crest of a wave, a safe and comfortable way of getting through angry waters. However, even a fast boat cannot always keep pace with the sweep of deep-sea wave systems. During a moderate summer blow on the North Atlantic, a typical wave—measuring 150 to 200 feet from crest to crest—travels at 20 knots; a storm comber 1,000 feet long races along at 40 knots.

Any boat overtaken by large, cresting breakers may get a cockpit full of water, or worse, it can be broached—swept sideways and possibly rolled over onto its beam-ends. Some have even been pitch-poled—tossed end over end. Fortunately, broaching and pitchpoling are rarities.

Nevertheless, a good seaman always keeps his eye on following seas, taking care to keep his stern square enough to the big ones so that they cannot broach his craft. Under severe conditions some experts recommend quartering—keeping the stern at a slight angle to an approaching wave, to expose less of the transom to the wave's force and to keep the stern from lifting so high that the bow digs in.

In a momentary lapse of attention, the skipper of the powerboat above has failed to keep his boat lined up with an overtaking wave. As a result, the wave is sluing the boat around broadside to the breaking crest. In this case the boat's inherent buoyancy keeps it from capsizing; but it could roll wildly and will probably have a cockpit full of water after the wave has swept by.

A Steadying Influence

The powerboat shown here has hoisted a steadying sail on a small mast so that the wind's pressure against it will minimize the roll of the boat in beam seas, and thus make steering easier. Such a sail is commonly rigged on a slow-moving, trawler-type boat. And if the boat's engine were to fail, the sail could be used to drive the boat slowly before the wind.

Running just ahead of a cresting comber, the boat above is correctly putting its quarter to the approaching wave. The sea will lift the stern, pass harmlessly under the boat and ease the craft comfortably into the following trough. The helmsman could then bear right or left according to his desired course until another big one comes up from behind.

Edging Through Squalls

Though generally slower and less maneuverable than a powerboat, a sailboat properly handled will find the going safe and reasonably comfortable even in heavy weather. The sailor, however, does have more work to do in dirty weather, and he is likely to spend more time enduring bad weather than the powerboatman, who can make a quick run for shelter.

When the wind begins to pipe up, a sailor's first task is to reduce his sail area. There are several methods of doing this, including reefing *(pages 106–107)* and actually taking in sails and setting smaller ones *(pages 108–109)*. In addition to these measures—or alternatively—a boat can carry an intentional luff in its sails when beating to windward, as at right. This simple tactic effectively reduces the working area of the sails, easing the strain on them and preventing the boat from being knocked down in the stronger gusts.

Carrying an intentional luff, however, should be only a temporary maneuver, used when the wind first strikes. A rising wind will inevitably bring bigger waves, especially in open water. The skipper of the boat at right has not only reduced sail by taking a reef in the main, but is employing careful helmsmanship, falling off the wind in the troughs, and then heading up into the wind in order to meet oncoming crests.

In a following sea, the sailboat skipper keeps his windward quarter—not his full stern—pointed toward the overtaking wind and waves to prevent the stern from being slued around so that an accidental jibe occurs.

By slacking his mainsheet slightly while maintaining headway with the jib, the skipper above has created a luff in his mainsail to ease the wind's pressure on it. This tactic helps keep the boat on its feet—that is, efficiently erect rather than heeled over so far that the leeward rail plunges under water.

Handling a sailboat in a rising head sea requires anticipation and timing, as illustrated here in the pictures and diagram. Sliding down the top of a wave *(above)*, this skipper heads off the wind slightly so as to hold his speed in the trough. As the next wave approaches and begins to lift the bow, he turns the boat slightly up into the wind *(above, right)* so as to meet the sea as close as possible to head on.

The diagram at left shows the path of the boat above as it is steered to windward through a steep sea—heading off through the troughs and heading up into the crests. Following such a weaving course keeps the boat moving along while preventing it from being caught broadside to a breaking wave.

Reefing the Main

In rising winds, when a sailboat heels 20° or more so that her leeward rail is consistently awash, the time has come to reef sail—and quickly. Most real trouble on open water comes not from the conditions, but from the boatman's failure to act quickly and with foresight. Good sailors, like those shown here, therefore, practice reefing and other foul-weather techniques on fair days, until their actions become second nature.

In recent years, two methods of reefing have come into widespread use, replacing less efficient traditional methods. One new technique is roller-reefing, in which sail area is reduced simply by rolling part of the mainsail around the boom. However, roller-reefing, though quick, tends to distort the sail, and the mechanism *(box, below)* requires regular maintenance. A more complex method is the jiffy reef, shown in sequence in the photographs at right.

Cranking In a Reef

In roller-reefing, the entire boom is rotated by a crank-and-gear mechanism like the one shown here. As the halyard is slowly eased, the sail rolls up around the boom in much the way a window shade wraps 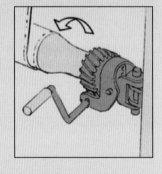 itself around its roller. The system does away with the need to lash the sail through cringles or with reef points because it is wrapped tightly around the boom. It also permits the crew to take in any desired amount of sail, not just the amount dictated by the placement of cringles.

The boatmen above have begun the process of jiffy-reefing. The sailor at the helm has eased the mainsheet to allow the boom to rise up, and to keep a slight luff in the mainsail. The crew has hauled the boom up to the leech cringle with a reef pendant, a line that runs from the port side of the boom up through the cringle, then down to a cheek block on the starboard side, from which it is led forward to a cleat on the boom.

In the second step in jiffy-reefing, the crewman at left in the picture below is slacking the main halyard while his mate pulls down on the reef pendant set in a luff cringle. This line, like the one in the leech cringle, runs from one side of the mast through the tack cringle and down to a cleat on the opposite side, where it will be secured when the sail has been lowered the proper amount.

In the left foreground *(above)*, the reef cringle on the luff has been secured to the boom. Crewmen have moved aft to furl the lowered part of the sail, folding and securing it by tying together lines called reef points set in pairs on opposite sides of the sail.

The crew completes the jiffy reef by securing the sail with quick, reliable reef knots—the seagoing name for the familiar square knot *(page 49)*. The helmswoman can now allow the boat to fall off the wind, trim the main and resume the original course.

Balancing in a Blow

In reducing sail a skipper must make sure to keep his sail plan balanced, so that the boat does not become hard to control. This may require putting up smaller sails or taking down some sails altogether.

To be in balance, the geometric center of the sail (called the total center of effort, or TCE) must be directly on the line of a boat's turning axis. A boat carrying too much sail forward in relation to sail area aft will tend to fall off the wind to leeward—a condition known as lee helm, and one that requires constant attention by the helmsman to avert an accidental jibe. Conversely, a boat carrying too much sail aft will constantly head up into the wind, and the helmsman will have to fight hard to keep on course. This latter condition is known as weather helm, and is dangerous only when it becomes excessive. In fact a slight degree of weather helm is desirable, for if the helm is momentarily eased, the boat will head up into the wind of its own accord.

To maintain balance as increasing wind forces him to take a reef or two in his mainsail, a skipper will usually have to compensate by putting on a smaller jib. As with reefing, the technique of changing headsails should be practiced on calm days. Under threatening conditions, the change should be made *before* the adjustment becomes absolutely necessary, and the maneuver should be carried out quickly and efficiently. The slippery, pitching foredeck of a sailboat can be a dangerous place during a blow and no one should be there longer than necessary; also, the boat may lose headway and maneuverability if it is too long without a headsail.

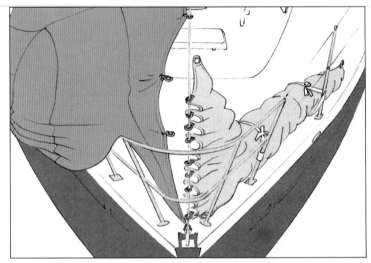

When changing jibs in rough weather, the first rule is to lash down the new jib, as shown above, to keep it from washing overboard. Then as soon as one or two bottom hanks of the hoisted jib have been undone, the new jib can be hanked onto the headstay. As one crewman lowers the hoisted jib, another finishes unhanking it. Finally, after rigging sheets, the crew members transfer the halyard, switch the tack fitting to the base of the new jib and haul it aloft.

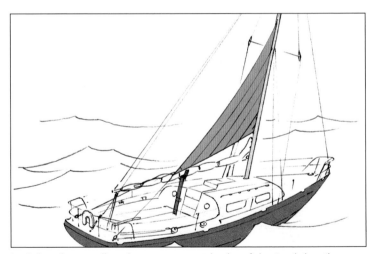

In winds too heavy to allow a boat to carry even a deeply reefed mainsail, the sailor may substitute a very small, heavy-duty trysail. The trysail may fit into the mainsail track, as above, or it may be fixed to the mast by rope rings strung with revolving wooden balls called parrel beads. The trysail's foot is not attached to the boom. The sail's sheets are led on either side of the boom to blocks on the boat's afterdeck, then forward to winches.

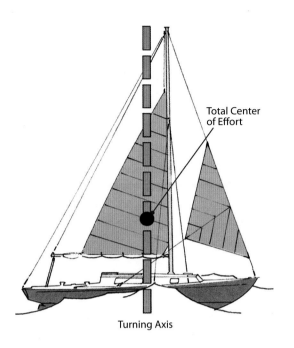

Total Center
of Effort

Turning Axis

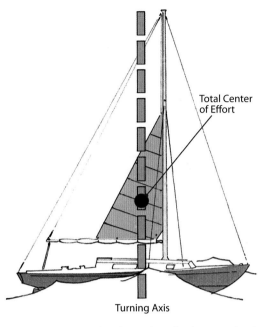

Total Center
of Effort

Turning Axis

Rigged at left with a single reef in the mainsail and a storm jib, and at right with a close-reefed main and no headsail, the sloop above is in perfect balance. In either case, the rig meets the requirement that the geometric center of the sail area (indicated by a dot) be directly on the boat's turning axis (shown with a broken line).

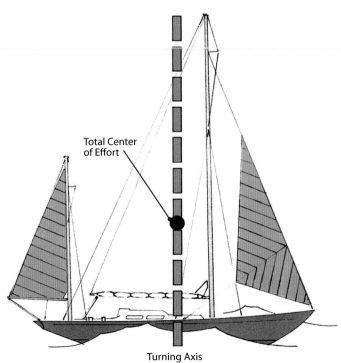

Total Center
of Effort

Turning Axis

Balancing sail for a heavy blow is perhaps easier on a yawl (or ketch) than on any other type of sailing craft. With mainsail furled, the yawl at left is riding under the so-called jib-and-jigger rig, which is composed of a working jib forward and a mizzen, or jigger, aft. The balance between the TCE and the turning axis remains approximately the same as it was before the mainsail was dropped.

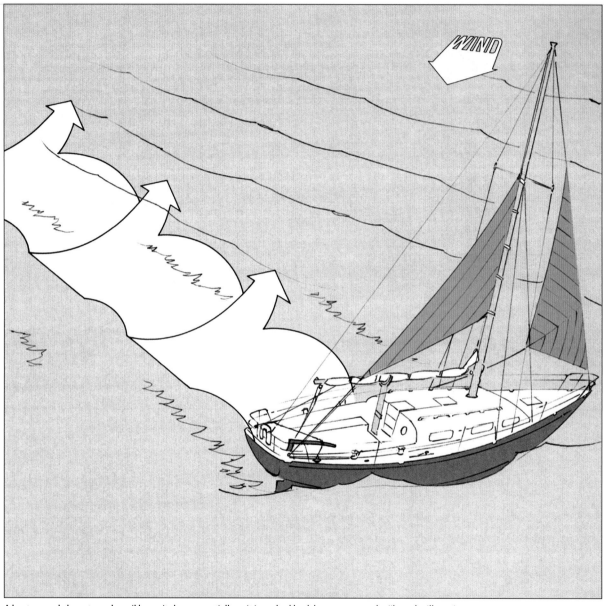

A boat properly hove to under sail keeps its bow essentially toward the oncoming waves, and maintains a relatively steady position though slowly making leeway. Aboard this sloop, a storm jib has been sheeted to windward, and the helm lashed to leeward. Under the pressure of the rudder, the boat will round up slowly to windward until it is pushed back by pressure on the jib, and will continue to follow this zigzag path without any help from skipper or crew. If the wind becomes so strong that it threatens to damage the sails and running rigging, the sails should be immediately struck and the boat hove to under bare poles, with the rudder still lashed to leeward.

Riding Out a Gale

When the wind and sea grow so violent that holding course is too dangerous or too exhausting, the time has come to stop fighting the elements and trim the ship so that it will take care of itself. This is most often done by the procedure called heaving to; a sound, well-equipped boat, properly hove to, can ride out a hurricane.

Sailboats and powerboats can be hove to in various ways, provided there is plenty of sea room and an offshore wind. A boat hove to makes some leeway and will eventually fetch up on the beach if the wind is onshore.

Depending on the wind's strength, a sailboat can heave to under sail or under bare poles, i.e., with all sails furled. A boat like the one at left, hove to under sail, responds alternately to the forces of wind and rudder, jogging up to windward, then falling off to leeward. If hove to under bare poles, with the tiller lashed to leeward, it will adhere, though more sluggishly, to the same rhythmic pattern.

Powerboats can be hove to by turning the bow to the oncoming wind and sea, and running the engine slowly to maintain the boat's position. Setting a sea anchor *(right)* achieves the same effect without burning fuel.

A boat can also ride out a storm by running before it; lines called warps, trailed astern, help to keep the boat from being slued around beam to the sea.

A powerboat caught in a storm with fuel running low can be hove to by setting a sea anchor off the bow with a bridle and a long hawser. The conical nylon sea anchor fills with water, and the resulting drag keeps the boat's bow to the sea. A trip line at the anchor's apex aids in hauling it aboard.

A canvas bag trailed astern, slowly leaking cod-liver or some other highly viscous oil, creates a slick that keeps approaching crests from breaking. An oil bag can be used in combination with other techniques—for example, on a line attached to a sea anchor.

Warps—long, heavy lines trailed astern of a boat running before a violent sea—will hold the boat's stern to the waves. This rarely used procedure (best when wave crests are breaking over the boat) requires a helmsman to keep the ship on a downwind course.

Challenging the Savage Sea

At some time in his life, despite careful planning and cautious forecasting, every man may fetch up against truly timber-shivering weather. The challenge can be both exhilarating and exhausting, a test punctuated with anxious moments and, occasionally, genuine crises. The skipper who sails skillfully and safely through an offshore gale may rightly feel himself the master of his ship.

The ocean-racing crews shown fighting the seas on these and the following pages are sailing along the fine line dividing calculated risk from reckless hazard. Their goal is to win, even if that means slugging it out for days on end with cresting seas in 50-knot winds. For example, during a race from Newport, Rhode Island, to Plymouth, England, the yawl *Ondine* carried her spinnaker for more than three days through winds gusting over 40—a gamble that cost more than one hair-raising knockdown but paid off with victory. In another transatlantic competition, the ketch *Alphard* found the wind so ferocious that the skipper hove to. When the wind dropped to a mere gale he set sail again for the finish line.

Occasionally, however, such daring insistence on keeping going can backfire, no matter how skilled the men aboard. The 50-foot sloop *Nepenthe* was dismasted in two successive Bermuda races, the first time because of faulty rigging, the next, when three huge waves in succession snatched up and then dropped the boat like a toy. On the last drop the specially strengthened rigging gave way, and *Nepenthe* was lucky to be rescued.

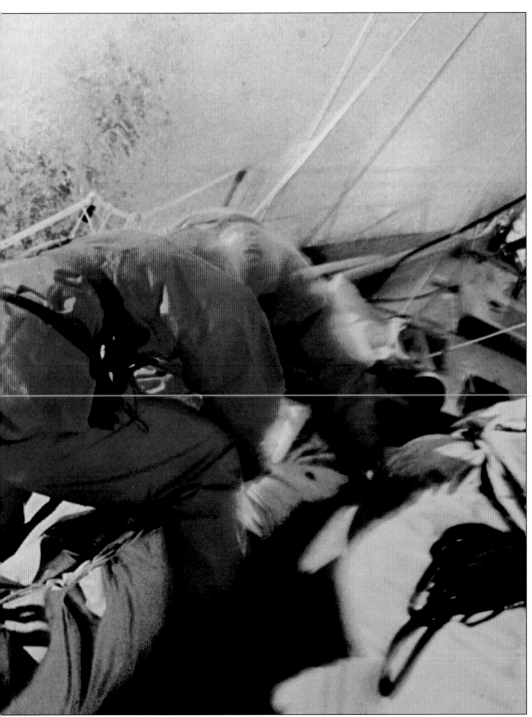

Two crewmen in bright orange foul weather gear struggle to secure a sail bag on the deck of an ocean racer during the 1973–1974 Whitbread Round-the-World Race. The man in the foreground has secured his safety harness to a life line—a rough-weather precaution that saved the lives of two crewmen of the ketch Sayula II who were washed overboard in the Indian Ocean during the same race.

Dealing with Foul Weather

Dealing with Foul Weather

The 57-foot yawl *Ondine* flings spray to leeward as a gust of wind knocks her down during the 1963 Transatlantic Race. Under such stormy conditions a cruising vessel would be under minimum sail, but *Ondine* continued to fly a spinnaker in 45-knot winds.

Mid-Atlantic spray cascades into the cockpit and drenches the helmsman of the yawl *Figaro III,* winner of a 3,500-mile race from Bermuda to Sweden. The angle of the gimbaled compass's face clearly shows the extent to which the yawl is heeling.

With her main and mizzen doused, the ketch *Melanie* rides under trysail and storm jib just off the Needles Channel that divides the Isle of Wight from the southern coast of England. Atop the mizzenmast, the British ensign snaps in gusts rising to over 50 knots. Below the flag is a radar reflector that was hoisted in the rigging to help larger vessels avoid running down the ketch in this rough weather.

CHAPTER 5:

When the Worst Happens

In the mind's eye of the novice skipper, his boat forever glides smoothly over the waters, hitting an occasional patch of rough weather, perhaps, but never running into serious trouble. While much of boating lives up to such romantic daydreams, nautical disasters occur, as the skipper of the boat on the opposite page learned to his sorrow. Similar incidents are commonplace in Coast Guard records.

Such misadventures may seem totally unavoidable, and some truly are—the Bailey family *(page 140)* could hardly anticipate that their sailboat would be stove in by a whale. The fact is, however, that beneath most marine disasters lies a history of oversight, overconfidence, or just plain carelessness. But once an emergency has struck, the cause matters far less than the solution; and every skipper should know how to meet—and minimize—the effects of fire, systems failures, and other accidents.

As a fundamental precaution, the skipper should keep on board a full tool kit *(page 129),* and he should check his emergency equipment regularly. He should always have a supply of fresh dry-cell batteries for flashlights and radio beacons. He should keep the first-aid kit freshly stocked. He should have a full complement of Coast Guard-approved fire extinguishers, and he should test them regularly according to the instructions on the labels.

Potential trouble spots should be checked routinely; for example, the strainers of the bilge pumps must be clear of debris. The seacocks for plumbing fixtures, whose pipe connections tend to develop leaks, must be closed when not in use. Even a luxuriously appointed yacht can gurgle to the bottom if the seacock for its head is inadvertently left open.

In addition to these routine precautions, the skipper should be prepared to take any action necessary to bring a damaged boat to shore. He should be ready to improvise repairs as amateur plumber, electrician, carpenter, or mechanic, using old cordage or pieces of canvas to block off a leaking hull, or rigging up an emergency steering system with a sail bag *(page 132)*. One skipper once used some nylon stockings as a replacement for a broken fan belt.

Above all, the boatman must be prepared to react appropriately in the case of dire emergency. He must know exactly what signals to use in calling for help. He should rehearse fire-fighting and man-overboard procedures. He should always have aboard one able-bodied and knowledgeable person to take his place if he is disabled. And he should know how to abandon ship and *when* to abandon ship.

A sailboat off the Oregon coast sank in shallow waters.

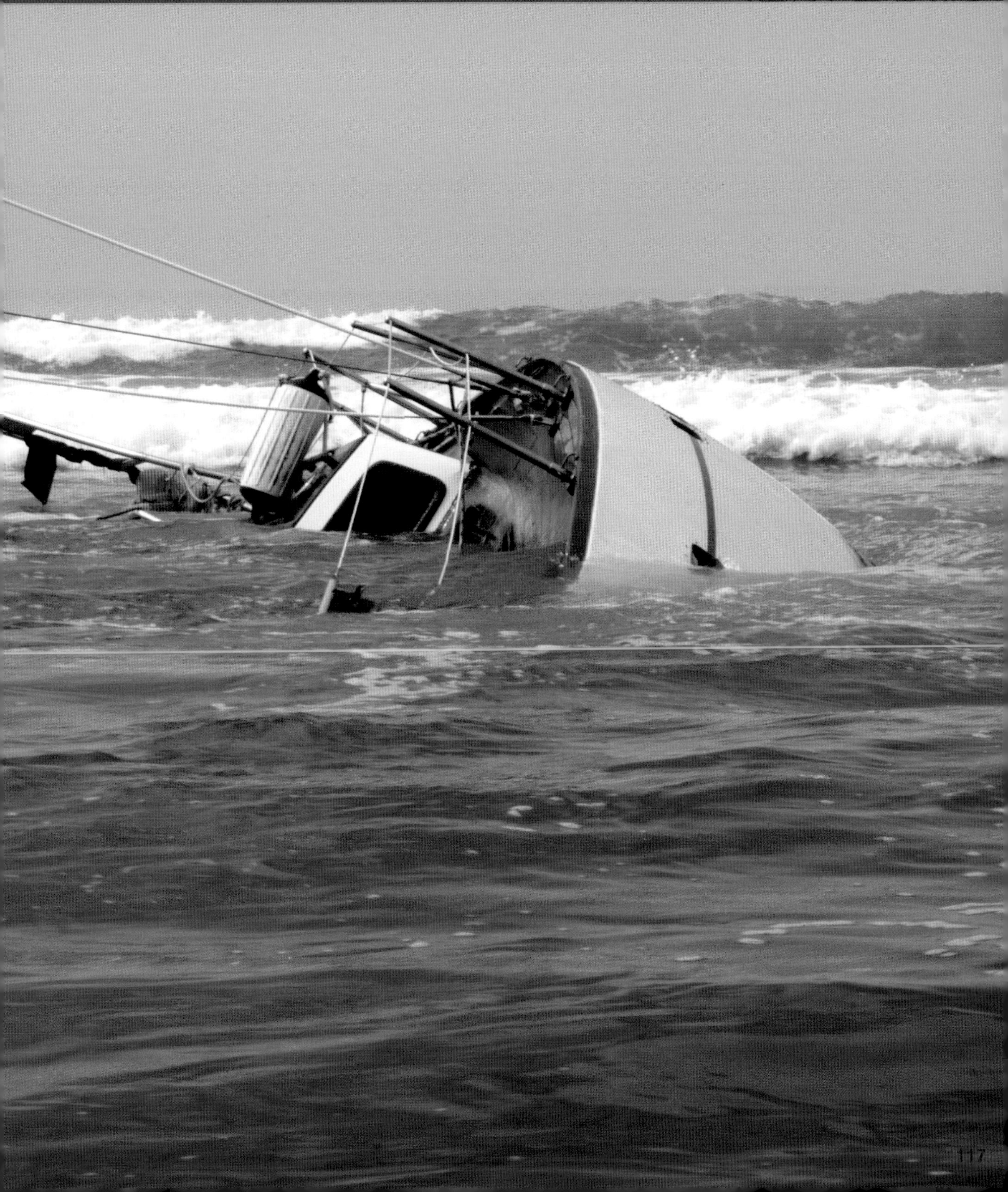

Signaling for Help

When trouble strikes at sea, a boat's captain should have two instantaneous responses: (1) go after the problem—or order someone else to do so; (2) call for help. And *never* hesitate to call for help. The Coast Guard would much rather arrive early to find all well than show up too late to help.

Another effective signal in open water is the international surface-to-air distress flag tied to the cabin roof *(above)*. Developed in Canada, this large panel of fluorescent orange cloth with black ball and square also catches the attention of surface craft if flown from a staff or rigging. Inshore in American waters, sailors still use the traditional distress sign of the U.S. ensign flown upside down.

In open water during daytime, dye marker stains the water yellow-green or orange to attract passing aircraft that can then radio for help. The dye usually comes as a powder; but do not simply shake it overboard, as the wind may scatter it. Instead, dissolve it in a can of seawater and empty the bucket slowly at water level. The stain, visible for 10 miles from the air, lasts 30 minutes in a calm sea.

Basically, any means of signaling that attracts attention is a good one. Use radio if you have it. Of any visual signals, the ones shown here have proved most effective. Each makes use of brilliant, eyecatching colors. The sudden glare of a red flare at night generates quick attention, and in daylight the vibrant stain of dye marker, the cloud of a smoke bomb or bright flashes of waving cloth will usually bring help in a short time.

Any boat that does not have radio should be equipped to give at least one daytime and one nighttime visual distress signal. But even on boats with radiotelephone *(pages 120–121)*, there ought to be some visual signaling equipment aboard in case power fails or the radio transmitter breaks down.

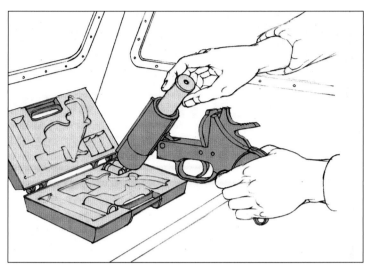

The most effective night signal is a flare, launched from a so-called Very pistol. Even by day these red flares can be used to summon rescuers. Load the pistol by pressing the barrel open and inserting a flare *(above)*; close it again.

The simplest visual distress signal, known to both sailors and airmen, is the age-old method of slowly and repeatedly raising and lowering your outstretched arms. To increase the chances of being seen, stand on the highest safe place on your boat and wave pieces of colored cloth or some shiny material such as aluminum foil.

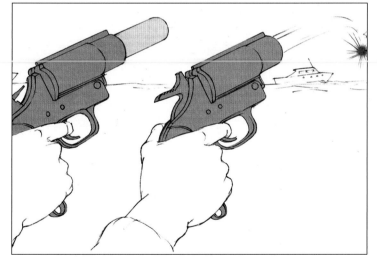

Cock the pistol by pulling the hammer back *(above, left)*; aim it up at a 45° angle, forward of any boat or plane in sight, and pull the trigger *(above, right)*. The parachute-held flare burns for 20 seconds, and on a clear night can be seen for 20 miles. Another type, without parachute, lasts six seconds. Hand-held flares can be seen for only a mile or so.

When the Worst Happens

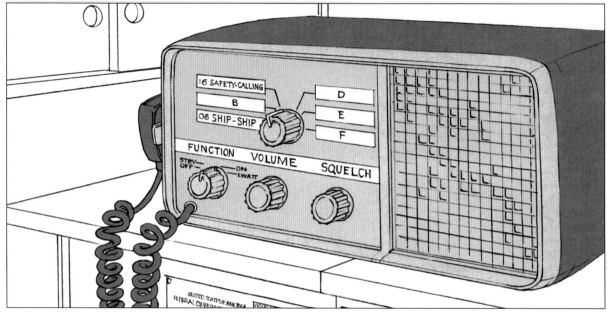

To send an emergency message on a radiotelephone, like the typical VHF-FM set shown above, switch the set on to full transmitting power. Turn the volume and squelch controls up and set the channel control to number 16, the emergency channel on all VHF-FM sets. The volume knob controls the loudness of incoming calls; squelch refines the incoming signal. Then broadcast your message, following the examples given on the opposite page. Post both operator and station licenses near the radio set, as required by the Federal Communications Commission.

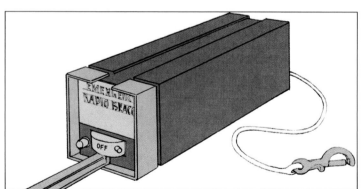

Boats without radiotelephone and those that cruise beyond the 20-mile range of shore stations should carry a battery-powered transmitter that broadcasts a distress signal over aviation emergency channels. Officially called an Emergency Position Indicating Radio Beacon, the nine-inch transmitter broadcasts continually for eight days (in storage, the batteries last up to 79 months), beaming a tone signal audible on receivers up to 200 miles away. Rescue craft with direction finders can home in on the signal even when the transmitter, designed to be buoyant, is afloat in its waterproof case.

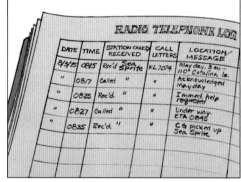

Keep a log book and at least two durable pens (in emergencies, pencils tend to break and single pens to go dry) by the radio, and immediately record incoming distress messages and your response, as shown here. This information must be available as the emergency develops, and cannot be trusted to memory, especially in times of stress.

Radio Distress Calls

The best way to get help in an emergency at sea is to broadcast a distress signal by radio. The Coast Guard and many civilian boats and planes constantly monitor radio distress frequencies. Sets range in sophistication and price from a compact emergency beacon to elaborate radiotelephone installations.

Although using a radiotelephone may seem complicated to the novice, these instruments are simple to operate. Every boatman owning a set should know how to send and receive distress calls before he leaves the dock so that his response to an emergency (box, right) will be immediate and confident.

If a genuine crisis should occur—sinking, fire, or acute illness—the boatman should send what is known as a "mayday" call (derived from m'aider, French for "help me"): the first word spoken is may-day. Mayday calls have first priority; and all other radio transmission stops when a mayday is heard. However, if life is not in immediate danger but help is needed—if you are out of gas, lost or run aground—send a "pan" call (from panne, French for "breakdown"). Pan calls have second priority. Important weather, navigation, and other marine safety information is preceded by the word "security."

Federal regulations require all new marine radio stations to use VHF-FM sets. But VHF-FM reception, though clear and reliable, is limited to a 20-mile range. Thus boats cruising farther offshore ought to carry an emergency beacon, which has a much longer range.

When life is in danger, begin a distress call with the word "mayday" repeated three times. Then transmit your radio call sign (i.e., station number) three times and your boat name three times. Follow with a full distress message, beginning again with "mayday" and next giving your call sign, boat name, location, conditions aboard and the identifying characteristics of your boat. For example: "Mayday. Mayday. Mayday. This is KL 7074. KL 7074. KL 7074. Sea Sprite. Sea Sprite. Sea Sprite." After a short pause, continue: "Mayday. KL 7074. Sea Sprite. Bearing one hundred and ten degrees true off Catalina Island. Distance about three miles. Fire out of control. Four persons aboard. May have to abandon ship. Vessel is thirty-foot cabin cruiser, black hull, white trim. Over." Then stand by for replies.

In a lesser emergency, when you need help but life is not in immediate danger, send a message patterned after the one given above, but use the word "pan" instead of "mayday".

The phonetic spelling alphabet is often the best means for spelling out radio call signs and any other words that may not be clearly understood. In the message above, the call sign could be spoken Kilo Lima 7074—and should be given this way if a repeat is requested.

A Alfa	**H** Hotel	**O** Oscar	**V** Victor
B Bravo	**I** India	**P** Papa	**W** Whiskey
C Charlie	**J** Juliett	**Q** Quebec	**X** X-ray
D Delta	**K** Kilo	**R** Romeo	**Y** Yankee
E Echo	**L** Lima	**S** Sierra	**Z** Zulu
F Foxtrot	**M** Mike	**T** Tango	
G Golf	**N** November	**U** Uniform	

If you hear a distress message, immediately stop any broadcast you may be sending. Listen to see if the message is answered. If it is not, then answer, giving the distressed vessel's call sign and name first and then your own. Follow this sequence: "KL [or Kilo Lima] 7074. KL 7074. KL 7074. Sea Sprite. Sea Sprite. Sea Sprite. This is WD [or Whiskey Delta] 4126. WD 4126. WD 4126. Mary Jane. Received mayday. Over." Pause for other stations to acknowledge the mayday call. Then offer assistance. If you are the closest vessel, let the distressed vessel know that you are proceeding to its aid and at what time you will probably arrive. Keep it informed of your progress and stay on the emergency channel until you are no longer needed.

A large sailboat quickly caught fire and burned after the mast came in contact with overhead electrical lines.

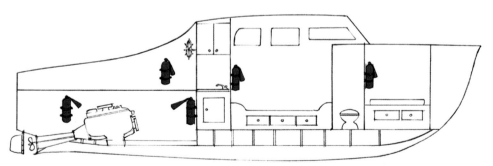

The best locations for fire extinguishers are shown here. At least one extinguisher, and more if space permits, should be permanently mounted on an engine-compartment bulkhead, and operated either by an automatic fire-sensing system or from on deck by remote control *(page 126)*. Another extinguisher, manually operated, should be near the stove. A third should be located at the helm. Auxiliary extinguishers are spotted where they can be reached quickly.

Fighting Fires While Afloat

Fire at sea is often a disastrous experience. If the flames are not quickly extinguished, skipper and crew may have no choice but to abandon ship. Boat fires generally originate from one of three sources: gasoline or diesel fumes, grease or fuel flare-ups from the galley stove, and faulty electric wiring. A careful skipper, therefore, shuts down fuel lines not in use and regularly checks all electrical circuits.

The handiest and most effective types of fire extinguishers for boats contain either CO_2 or halon gas, which smother a fire by cutting off its air supply, or dry chemicals that spray a powdery mist over the fire. Both types will snuff out most small fires, though gas works best in enclosed areas where the breeze will not blow it away.

Some boatmen favor foam extinguishers, but foam is messy to clean up and thus is less practical for minor blazes; and it may short-circuit exposed wiring. The landsman's favorite extinguisher—water—cannot be entirely relied on at sea, since it is ineffective against gasoline or oil fires.

Firefighter's Check List

If the blaze is from a loose object, such as a deck cushion or ashtray, toss it overboard immediately. If the fire is more serious, the skipper should:

- Close down fuel lines or electrical circuits related to or affected by the blaze.
- Maneuver the boat so that the wind carries the flames away from the cabin.
- Stop all forward motion to avoid fanning the flames.
- Localize the fire by closing all adjacent hatches, compartments and portholes.
- Use a fire extinguisher.

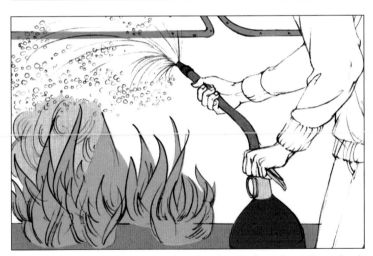

Foam fire extinguishers should be aimed not directly at the flames but at the overhead or at a bulkhead; the foam then sifts down over the flames, smothering them. With any extinguisher, proper application is vital—the flame-inhibiting blast of the commonest models lasts only eight to 20 seconds.

A dry-chemical or gas extinguisher must always be aimed at the base of the fire, where flames can be cut off at their source. To activate the extinguisher, pull the pin in the handle, freeing the trigger. Squeeze the trigger in spurts, sweeping the nozzle back and forth horizontally to arrest the flames.

When the Worst Happens

123

Hazard in the Galley

Most galleys are outfitted with alcohol stoves, which, while inexpensive, are designed in a way that occasionally makes them flare up. Luckily, such fires usually can be put out with a saucepan full of water *(right)*; unlike other liquid fuels, alcohol combines readily with water, thinning out so that it no longer burns. If the fire does not die immediately, however, it should be sprayed with a chemical extinguisher—which Coast Guard regulations require to be on an adjacent bulkhead. Galley curtains should be of fireproof fiberglass, and secured at the hem so that they do not billow over the stove.

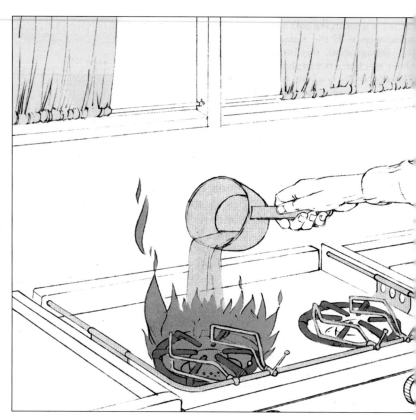

This diagram explains why alcohol stoves sometimes flare up. The burner transforms alcohol into a gas by heating it in a vapor chamber. First, the burner control knob is turned on, permitting liquid alcohol to flow into the priming pan. Then, with the knob off, the alcohol is lighted in the pan, starting a small fire that heats the burner—and the vapor chamber. When the knob is turned back on, the incoming alcohol is vaporized in the hot chamber, allowing only gas to escape. If the chamber has not been heated enough by the priming-pan fire, the alcohol remains liquid and flares up when ignited.

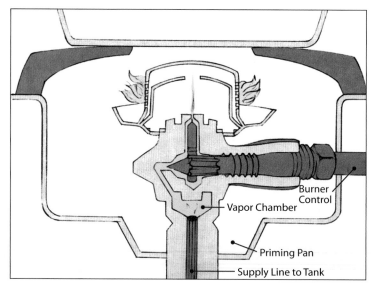

Burner Control

Vapor Chamber

Priming Pan

Supply Line to Tank

Precautions for Storing Stove Gas

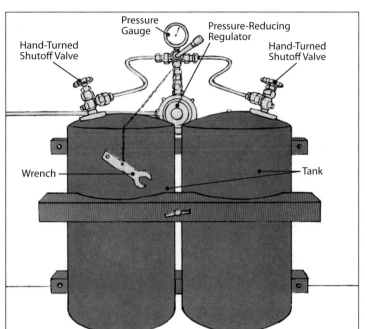

Pressure Gauge

Pressure-Reducing Regulator

Hand-Turned Shutoff Valve

Hand-Turned Shutoff Valve

Wrench

Tank

Another popular stove fuel that demands careful handling is tank-stored liquid petroleum gas (LPG), commonly propane or butane. For safety, each LPG tank should have its own hand-controlled shutoff valve, and there should be a pressure-reducing regulator and gauge to monitor gas flow, and a special wrench to fit the tanks' fittings. The tanks must be stored above decks in a well-ventilated compartment with a hatch (lower picture) so that leaking fumes will be carried away. Signs listing precautions and instructions for LPG use should be posted near the tanks and also near the galley stove.

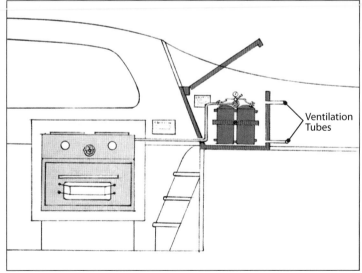

Ventilation Tubes

Fuel and Engine Fires

An extinguisher permanently mounted in the engine compartment and touched off by remote control, allows a helmsman to quell a blaze without leaving the wheel and losing control of the boat. The extinguisher may be loaded with CO_2, halon gas, or dry chemicals—all suitable for smothering gasoline or oil fires. The engine-room hatch must be kept closed so that no air enters to dissipate the extinguishing agent or feed the flames. Remote systems such as the one shown are so effective that boats equipped with them may qualify for lower insurance rates.

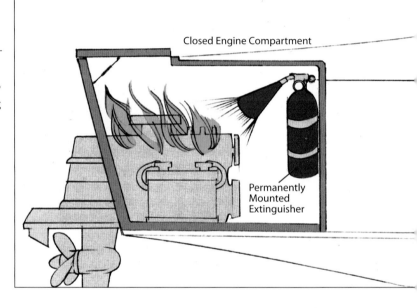

Closed Engine Compartment

Permanently Mounted Extinguisher

A fuel tank and its compartment require ventilation and securing devices to reduce fire hazard. Steel straps lash the tank solidly to the boat's structure, and an interior baffle keeps the fuel from sloshing around. A flexible fuel intake tube gives with the stress motions that occur in any boat. Large vents blow fresh air through the fuel compartment to carry away fumes. A smaller vent inside the tank allows excess fuel to spill harmlessly overboard, carries off fumes and admits air to compensate for changes in fuel levels. Ground wires from the tank to the bonding system render sparks harmless.

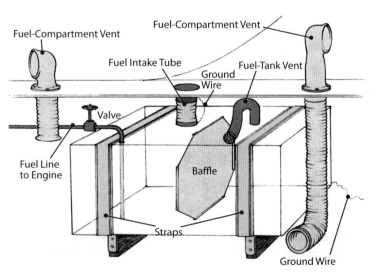

Fuel-Compartment Vent

Fuel-Compartment Vent

Fuel Intake Tube

Ground Wire

Fuel-Tank Vent

Valve

Fuel Line to Engine

Baffle

Straps

Ground Wire

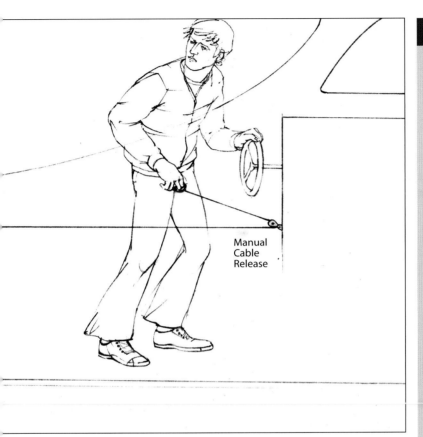

Manual Cable Release

The Threat of Lightning

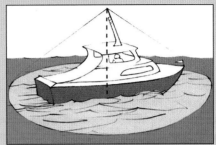

Though lightning seldom strikes a boat's hull, it sometimes hits the top of the mast. From there it vents its force within a cone that extends about 60° on either side of the mast and usually includes most of the boat. Within this cone the destructive force is awesome; a wood mast can be snapped off, and the lightning may rip into the boat itself and even set it ablaze. (Metal masts and boats are less hazardous, since they ground lightning automatically.) To transform the cone of destruction into a cone of protection, experienced seamen ground their wood masts by installing a metal rod at the tip and running a cable to a grounding bolt in the keel.

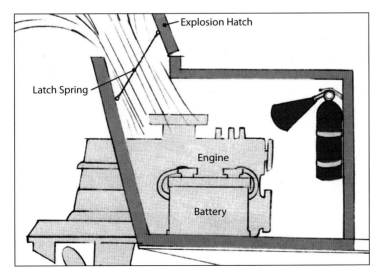

Explosion Hatch

Latch Spring

Engine

Battery

An explosion hatch designed by the Coast Guard directs the force of an engine-compartment blast away from the cabin and crew. If a spark from the engine ignites fuel fumes, or even the hydrogen gas given off by the battery, the blast forces open the explosion hatch. After the explosion, a powerful latch spring pulls the hatch back into place to prevent oxygen in the outside air from feeding the fire that almost immediately follows such explosions.

In 1974 the sloop *Bohemia* was dismasted in San Francisco Bay when her spinnaker pole dipped into a wave; the strain snapped the mast. A crew member *(foreground)* dived under the boat to free the lines fouling the propeller and rudder, and the *Bohemia* returned to the dock under power. Had she lacked an engine, her crew could have jury-rigged and sailed home, as described on page 139.

Dealing with Damage

When a drifting log suddenly punctures a boat's hull or a mast crashes over the side *(left),* those aboard must move quickly and effectively to save the boat and themselves. There are ways and means for dealing with practically the whole range of boating emergencies. Any of them can be a lifesaver or, at the least, a boat saver.

In an emergency, the skipper may have to improvise to match the circumstances. But experts agree that the best way to meet any nautical crisis is beforehand, when the skipper has time to prepare for the unexpected. The most effective antidote to disaster is constant inspection of the boat from masthead to rudderpost, to reveal the worn turnbuckle, the frayed fan belt, or the propeller shaft that will let go when least expected.

Equally important is adequate emergency equipment. No matter how constantly a boat is inspected, the stresses that occur at sea can at any moment overwhelm wood and metal. A spare propeller or even a cork costing less than a dime for plugging a seacock can make the difference between a tragic and a happy ending to a cruise. The collection of gear at right includes these and other common items.

Most important is a calm attitude that both anticipates trouble and seeks solutions. Time spent ashore contemplating what to do if the hull is stove in or the rig collapses can prepare all hands to perform like the crewmen on the opposite page; though they lost both their mast and the race, they sailed home safely.

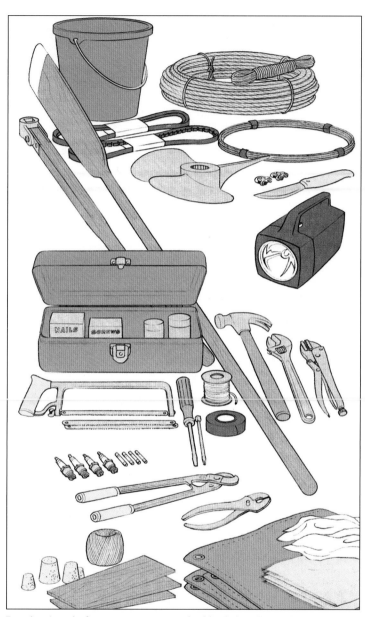

Every boat's stock of emergency equipment should include such crucial spare parts as those shown above. They include: an auxiliary tiller (top left, next to oar), fan belts, as well as wire rope and U-bolts (under the rope coils). Small, easily lost items—fuses, spark plugs, electrical wire, cotter pins, shear pins and turnbuckles—can be stowed in a box *(center, left)*. In addition, the boatowner is wise to keep scrap wood, corks, stout twine, and a tarpaulin *(bottom)* for making repairs.

Keeping the Water Out

Though the primary function of any hull design is to keep the water out, some water is deliberately passed through the boat for sinks, heads, and engine cooling. This water leaves and enters by means of carefully designed apertures called through-hull fittings. And these fittings, when near or below the waterline, are equipped with valves called seacocks. Made of plastic or metal, seacocks open and close with the turn of a handle. Should the fitting itself—or the hose attached to an open seacock—rupture or become loose, water will pour into the boat.

The skipper must know the location of the seacocks, close them when the boat is not in use and test them regularly to make sure they open and close easily. He should also keep a few corks on board for emergency repairs *(right, bottom).*

Once a boat has taken on unwanted water, the skipper should bail it out as soon as possible, using one of the types of bilge pumps shown here. Many inboard-powered boats have an electric pump in the engine compartment or a hand pump permanently mounted near the helm. A portable hand pump should also be carried for emergency duty anywhere on the boat *(opposite, bottom).* And as extra insurance in the event of pump failure, every skipper should learn how to jury-rig an engine's cooling system to move water from the bilges *(right, top).*

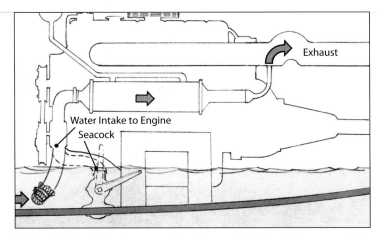

If the regular electric bilge pump on an inboard-powered boat breaks down, an engine's water-cooling system can be turned into an improvised bilge pump. First, the engine's water-intake seacock is closed. Then the intake's hose clamp is loosened and the hose's end freed to dangle in the water. A jury-rigged strainer made of window screening should be tied or clamped to the hose's end. When the engine is turned on, water will be sucked through the hose and pumped out with the exhaust *(arrows).*

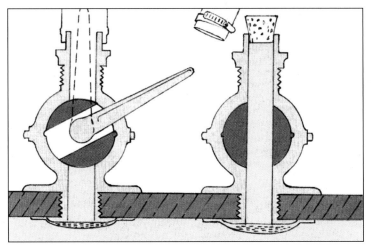

A seacock is a valve designed to control the flow of water through the hull. Basically it is an expanded section of pipe containing a ball valve that can be opened or closed by a straight handle. A quarter turn with the handle moves the solid sides of the ball over the pipe's entry and exit passages, closing them off *(right).* With the handle in the upright position *(dotted line),* a channel through the ball allows water to pass through the seacock. If corrosion causes the seacock to freeze at the open position and its connecting hose comes off, water will pour into the boat. To halt the water, a cork can be inserted *(far right)* to stop the flow until the seacock can be repaired in port.

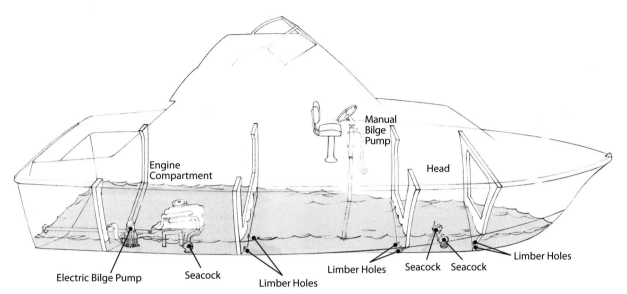

Engine
Compartment

Manual
Bilge
Pump

Head

Limber Holes

Electric Bilge Pump

Seacock

Limber Holes

Limber Holes

Seacock   Seacock

Limber Holes

Typical placement for bilge pumps and seacocks is shown in this schematic drawing. A manual pump is fixed by the helm. An electric pump takes water from the engine compartment. This compartment also has a seacock through which the engine draws water as a coolant. The head has two seacocks for the toilet—one for intake and the other for discharge. Many boats are now equipped with catch tanks, where waste water is chemically treated before being discharged, since pumping toilets directly into the water is unlawful in some states. Note that the boat's bulkheads are notched with so-called limber holes, allowing water to flow toward the hull's lowest parts.

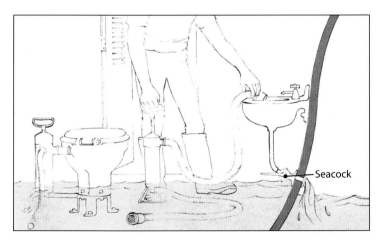

Seacock

When through-hull fittings start to leak or the connecting hose on an open seacock breaks, flooding can occur, sometimes in parts of a boat not served by automatic pumps. Here, a portable bilge pump is used to draw water from the floor of a head and spew it into the basin, where it runs down a drain and through a seacock. Though powerboat drains are normally well above the waterline where seacocks are unnecessary, this low-placed one has a seacock—as would any sailboat.

When a boat springs a serious leak or has a hole stove in its hull, skipper and crew have to move fast—and know what to do. First they should shore up the hole from the inside and get the pumps going. If the leak is bad enough, they must then cover it from the outside by actually wrapping the damaged section with stout cloth, as shown here. The crew members of this powerboat have removed the canvas cockpit canopy from its frame. Tying its rear corners to deck cleats above the hole, they then fasten lines to the other corners and work them under the hull, finally securing these lines, too, onto the far side of the boat. If the crippled craft were a sailboat, a jib—or even the mainsail if need be—would serve as a hull wrapping. Although this hull is wooden, the plug-and-wrap method of covering a hole works equally well on fiberglass or metal boats.

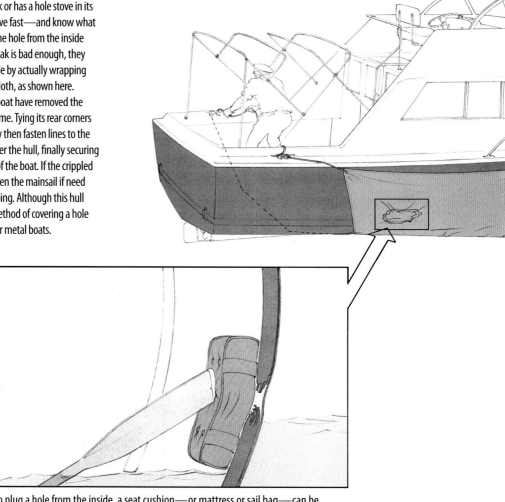

To plug a hole from the inside, a seat cushion—or mattress or sail bag—can be pressed over it. An oar, mop handle or floorboard is then wedged between the cushion and some convenient brace to keep the seal in place. If no means for bracing exists, a crew member should hold the cushion.

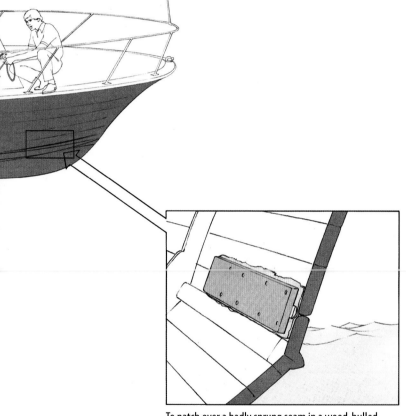

To patch over a badly sprung seam in a wood-hulled boat, take some flexible material like a piece of canvas and cover it with epoxy glue or some other handy sealant before pressing it over the seam. Then roll up another piece of canvas, or a rag or sponge rubber, place it over the treated fabric and nail it all down.

To keep a hole in its hull above the waterline, this sailboat is deliberately heeled over as far as it can safely go. To maintain the boat at this extreme angle, its sails are kept close-hauled, and the crew hikes out on the leeward side of the boat.

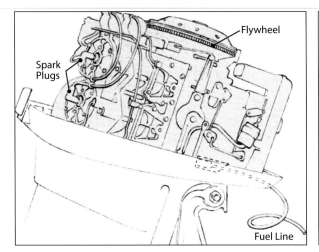

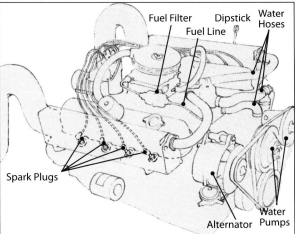

Troubleshooter's Check List

The drawings above show most of the parts of an outboard *(left)* and an inboard engine to which, in case of a breakdown, the average boatman can apply the emergency remedies outlined below.

Problem: starter motor works but engine doesn't

	Steps Toward Solution
Engine not getting fuel	Check the fuel supply. Make sure the fuel-line valve and fuel-tank vent are open. Inspect the fuel line for leakage. Wrap any breaks with tape. Unclog any filters between the fuel supply and the engine. On some inboards, a filter plug can be removed to let sediment drain out. On others the filter must be disassembled and the filtering element cleaned. On outboards, remove the fuel-line assembly from the tank and clean the strainer.
Engine flooded	After letting the engine sit for about half an hour with the ignition off, crank the engine several times with the throttle and the manual choke, if the engine has one, both fully open. Then try restarting the engine.
Engine overheats	Let the engine cool before restarting. If it reheats rapidly, as shown by an inboard's temperature gauge or by heat waves emanating from an outboard, let the engine cool again. Feel around the engine's cooling-water intake and remove any debris clogging it. On inboards, tighten the water-pump belt if it is loose; if it is broken, replace it—with a jury-rigged spare if necessary. Check the cooling-water hoses for breaks. Check the lubricating oil supply with the dipstick and add oil if necessary. On inboards with closed cooling-water systems, check the tank holding the circulating fresh water and add water if necessary.
Wet or defective wiring	Clean all dirty connections, tighten loose ones, dry off wet ones. Mend or replace loose, broken, frayed or corroded wires, if necessary using a length cut from a less vital part of the boat's electrical system.

Lack of spark	Remove the wire from one spark plug. With the end of the wire one quarter inch from the engine block, crank the engine over. (Or remove the plug, reconnect it to the wire and lay the spark-plug threads against the block.) No spark—or a weak (yellow) one—indicates that repairs must be made in port. A strong (blue) spark means the ignition system is functioning up to the point where current enters the plugs: check each plug.
Defective spark plugs	Dry the upper tips of the plugs and the wire-end connections. Then try starting the engine. If it still does not start, remove the plugs, clean them if they are fouled; replace any damaged ones.
Problem: Starter does not work	**Steps Toward Solution**
Discharged or low battery	Turn off lights or other equipment that may be drawing current. Give the battery 30 minutes to recover. Meanwhile, remove the battery cable connections, clean the posts and connections, and reclamp them firmly together. Check each battery cell. If no water is visible, fill with fresh—and preferably distilled—water. On inboards, tighten the belt from the drive shaft to the alternator if it is loose. If it is broken, replace it.
Defective starter switch	Check all connections for tightness; repair broken wires by drawing together their raw ends and then tightly taping over the repair. Cover with tape any piece of wire or connection that is exposed to moisture.
Defective solenoid	Turn on the starter switch and listen for the distinctive click a solenoid makes when working properly. If no click comes, the solenoid is broken, probably beyond the repairing ability of all but a skilled mechanic.

When the Worst Happens

Restoring Power

Since even the best of marine engines may break down in mid-voyage, there are a number of steps a boatman can take to get his motor going long enough to reach port.

By far the commonest cause of marine-engine failure is running out of gas. Every skipper should know his engine's average per-hour consumption of gas, and should always top off his tanks before leaving the dock.

Clogged fuel lines and ignition problems can usually be cured with a spark-plug wrench or one of the other tools and spare parts shown on page 129. When the engine fails, turn off the ignition and pocket the key to preclude accidental starts or shocks from live wires. Drop the anchor and take time for careful repairs. Let the engine cool; overheating may be the basic problem.

First remove an outboard engine's cover or an inboard's hatch cover. Often the trouble will be quickly apparent—a loose wire or a broken belt. Manufacturers even anticipate some of the commonest problems. For example, most outboards will come equipped, in case the electric starter fails, with a manual starter—a cord fitted with a handle and wrapped around a notched collar on the flywheel. If the cord is lost or broken, any light line will serve. A length of line also can substitute for a belt on an inboard engine *(top right)*. On most outboards, a damaged propeller *(right)* or shear pin can be replaced by a spare. A burst hose can be taped.

If in doubt about the location or appearance of a part, consult the owner's manual. After completing a repair, put the clutch in neutral before restarting the engine; replace the engine cover before resuming the trip. And if repair is impossible, never be ashamed to signal for help.

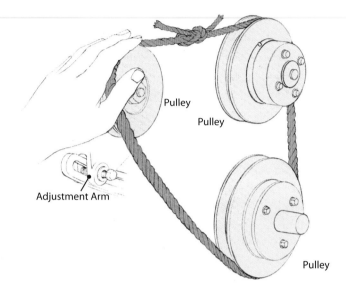

Pulley
Pulley
Adjustment Arm
Pulley

In a pinch, a length of line can be made to substitute for a broken belt on an inboard engine. First loosen the adjusting arm located next to one of the pulleys on which the belt is mounted. Tie the line around the pulleys with a square knot, then retighten the adjusting arm, making the jury-rigged belt as tight as possible. The substitute belt will slip and will soon wear out, but if the engine is run slowly the line may last long enough to get the boat back to port.

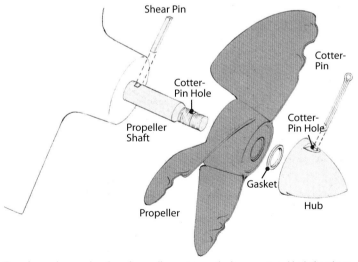

Shear Pin
Cotter-Pin
Cotter-Pin Hole
Cotter-Pin Hole
Propeller Shaft
Gasket
Hub
Propeller

To replace a damaged outboard propeller, swing up the lower unit and lock the tilting mechanism. Pull out the cotter pin and unscrew the hub. Remove the gasket behind the hub. Pull off the propeller. Replace the shear pin if it is damaged. Push the new propeller onto the shaft, replace the gasket, and screw on the hub until the cotter-pin holes in the hub and shaft are aligned. Replace the pin.

Steering Failure

Loss of steering is one of boating's most unnerving emergencies. When it occurs, the skipper, if running on power, should put his engine into neutral. If under sail, he should head into the wind. His object is to slow the boat until he can assess the trouble and devise a solution.

With luck, he will find the rudder intact, with damage done only to the tiller, or in more complex steering mechanisms, to the cable and pulleys that connect the wheel to the rudder. A spare tiller should always be carried on any boat. If it is broken or missing, the crew can fashion a temporary tiller or make the other running repairs shown right. And if the rudder itself has gone, an ingenious boatman can rig a jury rudder of one kind or another.

One recourse is available to a skillful sailboat crew that is denied to those on a powerboat: they can steer with their sails alone, alternately trimming and slacking the jib and main to move the bow onto or off the wind.

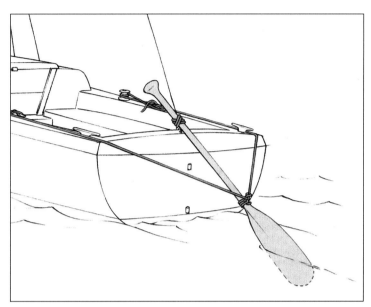

To rig a jury rudder with an oar, form a steering bridle by tying a line around the oar as close as possible to the blade, using a rolling hitch secured with a half hitch. Cleat the ends of the bridle to either side of the boat. Place the oar as far out as possible to increase leverage and lash it to the backstay. The bridle, which should be kept taut by pressure on the oar, can now be trimmed to set direction.

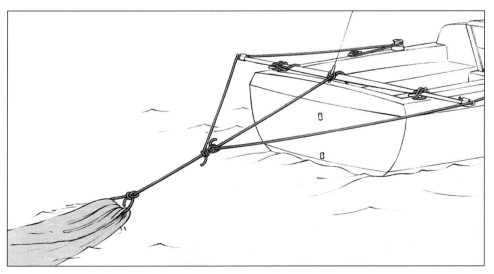

For an alternate emergency steering gear, a drag—a tire, sea anchor, or (as here) a sail—will provide a measure of control. Attach the drag to the stern with a line. Using rolling hitches, tie two other lines to the first and lead them around a spinnaker pole. Lash the pole across the stern, cleat the two lines, throw the drag out and trim as required.

Repairing the Rig

Aboard a well-maintained sailboat, the rigging rarely fails. But if it does, the effect may range from the mere inconvenience of a parted sheet to disastrous damage to the standing rigging. Under sail, if a shroud or a stay begins to go, immediately turn the boat so the force of wind on the sails is shifted to undamaged rigging. A weak port shroud, for example, can be kept from parting by putting the boat on the starboard tack. And if the shroud has already broken, prompt action may save the mast.

When standing rigging fails, it must be repaired at once. The simplified drawing on this page shows two methods for fixing a severed stay; either would work just as well on a shroud. The opposite page shows one way to jury-rig after a dismasting. But there is no single "right" way to jury-rig; a spinnaker pole, rather than an oar, might serve as a temporary mast. The seaman must improvise a rig, using available materials, so that he can hoist a sail.

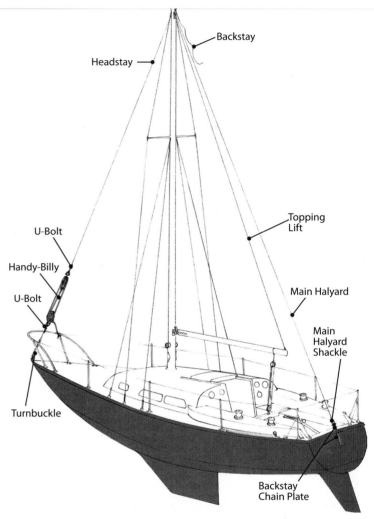

A temporary stay can be made of a halyard—shown here replacing the backstay. When the backstay parts, immediately head into the wind so that the wind's force presses aft on the mast. Quickly sheet the boom hard amidships; this causes the mainsail leech to act with the sheet as a temporary backstay. Then tighten the topping lift to provide additional staying force. After lowering the jib and the main, shackle the main halyard to the backstay chain plate and pull the halyard tight with its winch.

If a stay breaks within a crewman's reach, he can repair it with a handy-billy, as has been done with the headstay above. To make this repair, the instant the stay lets go, turn the boat directly downwind, taking all forward strain off the mast. Leave the main up with the boom well out. Rig an extra jib or spinnaker halyard as a temporary headstay. Then let the jib down; make a loop in each of the stay's severed ends and secure them with U-bolts.

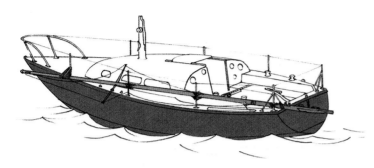

The first task after a dismasting—once all the crew is accounted for—is to get control of the broken spar so it cannot punch through the hull. In a moderate sea, the crew may be able to lash the mast tightly to the deck *(left)*. In rough water, the entire rig must be cast away to prevent hull damage. Wire shrouds and stays, frequently too tough for wire cutters, can be detached at the turnbuckles. Though a wood mast tends to break completely, remnants of an aluminum mast may have to be sheared off with wire cutters or a hacksaw. Try to salvage sheets and halyards; they are invaluable for jury-rigging.

A new mast can be rigged from an oar secured by shrouds and stays made from jib or spinnaker lines. After cutting four lengths of line, tie one end of each to the oar handle with a clove hitch secured by a half hitch. Then lash the oar to the stump of the mast. Reeve the new shrouds through the chain plates on deck, using shackles if necessary to prevent chafing, and adjust the shrouds to hold the oar vertical. Fasten the headstay to the stem fitting (or to a mooring cleat), then pass the backstay through the stern chain plate and tighten it to keep the oar upright.

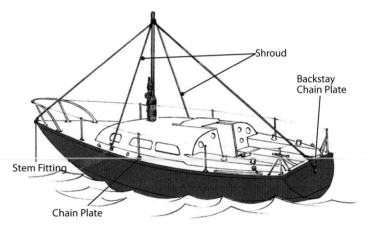

Shroud

Backstay Chain Plate

Stem Fitting

Chain Plate

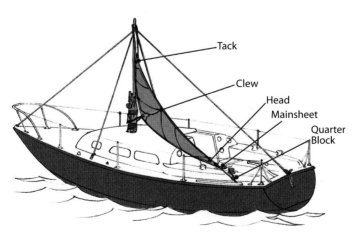

Tack

Clew

Head

Mainsheet

Quarter Block

While almost any small sail can be bent to the new mast, the best sail to use is the heavy-duty storm jib, whose foot becomes the luff in the new rig. Tie the tack of the jib (now the head) to the mast above the shrouds and stays so it will not slide down. Fasten the clew (now the tack) to the base of the mast below a cleat, or with several turns of line, to keep the sail from riding up. Then attach the mainsheet to the head of the jib (now the clew), reeve it through the quarter block and take it around a winch to trim the sail.

When the Worst Happens

Casting off the rubber dinghy he has just launched, skipper Maurice Bailey glances toward his wife, Maralyn, as their sloop, *Auralyn*, sinks into the Pacific. *Auralyn* had been stove in by a sperm whale, and despite the Baileys' efforts to plug the hole, the boat was gone minutes after Mrs. Bailey took this picture. Using the dinghy and a rubber life raft they also managed to launch, the Baileys stayed constantly afloat until rescued—1,500 miles away from the sinking.

Survival at Sea

Without warning, a man tumbles overboard and is rapidly left astern. Or just as suddenly, a boat rams a submerged object, fills and starts to sink. Fortunately, such heart-stopping crises are rare. But they *do* occur, and every seaman must be ready to heave a horseshoe buoy like the one at right, launch a raft *(page 145)* or climb into a helicopter's rescue basket.

Cool-headed mariners like Maurice Bailey, an English yachtsman *(left),* photographed by his wife as they abandoned their sinking craft in mid-Pacific, have survived because they had prepared themselves with survival gear and the knowledge to use it. The Baileys very quickly launched a rubber dinghy and a life raft, and packed each with food, water, and other essential supplies. The one item they had forgotten was fishing gear, but Mrs. Bailey made hooks out of strong safety pins from a first-aid kit. They caught and ate fish, using leftovers as bait to catch more fish, and also turtles. One hundred and nineteen days after the sinking, the Baileys, gaunt but still healthy, were picked up by a passing vessel.

Advance preparation and swift actions are just as essential in a man-overboard situation. When it occurs, whoever spots the victim instantly shouts "Man overboard!" and throws over a flotation device. Someone should keep him constantly in sight.

Simultaneously, the helmsman checks his watch and compass and prepares to swing his boat onto a return course. The crewman who throws the flotation gear, preferably a life preserver equipped with survival gear like the one at right, should take care to heave it upwind

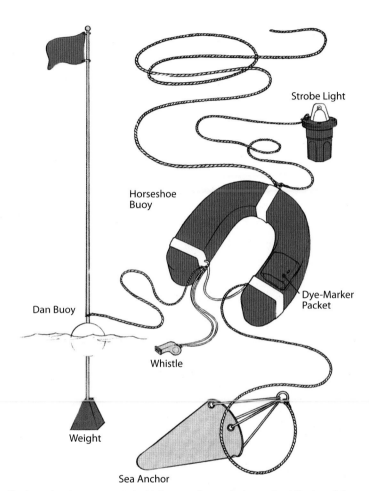

Strobe Light

Horseshoe Buoy

Dye-Marker Packet

Dan Buoy

Whistle

Weight

Sea Anchor

The horseshoe buoy, connected with lines to other survival gear, should be tossed the moment a man goes overboard. The horseshoe supports the victim, and the dan buoy, weighted so that its flag flies upright, makes him easier to spot, especially in rough seas. Other items are orange or yellow-green dye for release in the water, a whistle, and a strobe light that goes on when it hits the water and can be seen for miles at night. The sea anchor reduces drifting.

and upcurrent of the man in the water so that it will drift toward him. Even if the swimmer is unable to reach the preserver, it will mark the area of his last known position. And, if he reaches it, he can remain afloat for hours if his friends lose sight of him and have to launch a search pattern to find him and pick him up.

Search and Pickup

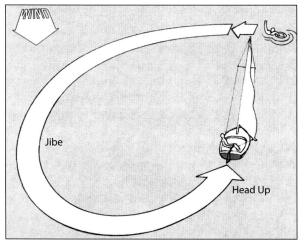

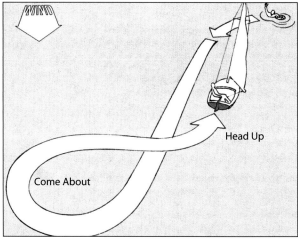

The fastest way to retrieve a man who has fallen overboard is to jibe, then circle back into the wind and bring the boat to a stop to weather of the man. The helmsman or crew can then proffer a hand, a line, or a boathook.

In heavy weather, the best pickup plan is to bear off briefly, then come about to cross the former course before heading up just to weather of the swimmer. The hull will shield the man in the water from wave action.

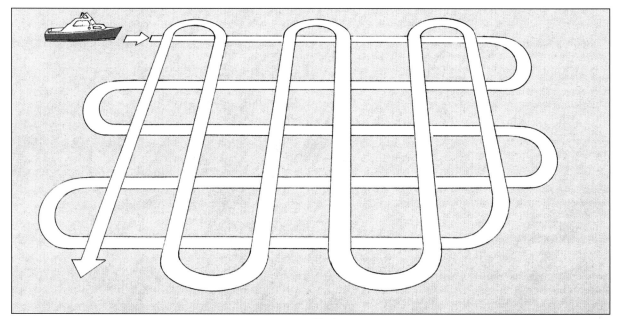

At night, in fog or in choppy seas, a man overboard may drift quietly out of sight. In such cases, the skipper should instantly lay a course toward the man's last position, then begin crisscrossing the area in a pattern

like that shown above, with a lookout posted as high up on the vessel as possible. By sticking to this method, one skipper in a transpacific race rescued a man lost overboard 20 hours earlier.

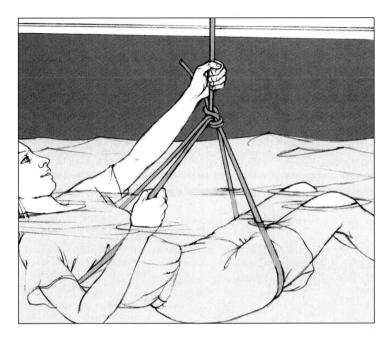

When a person overboard is too weak or heavy to be hauled in by hand, a bowline on a bight *(left)*, secured to the mainsheet, makes a good rig for helping the rescued one aboard. Rescuers begin by heaving a line with a loop in the end that the person can grab to be drawn to the ship's side. Then the swimmer wriggles into the bowline's double loops. The crew stays aboard unless the person rescued is unconscious or in imminent danger of drowning. A shipmate who leaps into the water to help doubles the number of people to be rescued and reduces the number of effective crew members aboard.

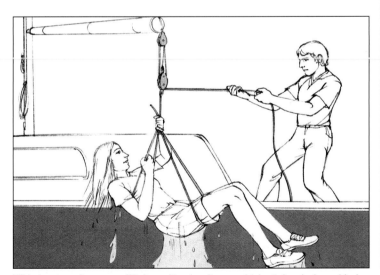

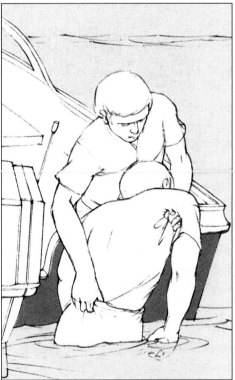

With the rescued person well balanced in a bowline on a bight tied to the lower block of the mainsheet purchase, a crewman hauls his shipmate back aboard. If possible, another crewman should steady the boom. The person overboard can aid importantly in his own rescue by staying calm, shedding heavy clothing and floating quietly rather than exhausting himself by frantic—and futile—swimming.

A person overboard reentering a small boat, whether clambering in by himself or being hauled aboard as here, should make his entry over the stern. Any attempt to get aboard amidships or over the bow can end in a capsize; and in rough water a plunging bow may knock a swimmer unconscious.

Refuge on a Raft

For any boat that occasionally ventures offshore from coastal waters or on the Great Lakes, where getting lost can mean days on open water, a heavy-duty life raft like that shown here can be vital to survival. Most cruising boats also carry or tow a conventional dinghy. But dinghies are not designed to carry people for any length of time, and tend to capsize easily. A well-designed raft, however, can last for months in mid-ocean.

A typical life raft is made of a heavy rubberized fabric in a bright, attention-getting color, and includes a permanently attached canopy to protect the crew from the elements. A CO_2 bottle quickly inflates the raft's air chambers—either of which can keep a fully loaded raft afloat.

The raft must be instantly available in some above-deck place like a seat locker. And the boatman should determine at the time of purchase that the raft's container holds the gear shown opposite. For long-term survival, there are certain additional items *(right)* that should be included. Perishable materials such as food, medicines, and flares must be checked and replaced regularly.

Ideally, the raft should be tested in water when purchased, but this is frequently impractical. In any event, it should be checked annually thereafter to make sure all its components are working properly. It must then be repacked by a professional whose skills are as vital to the raft's crew as a parachute rigger's are to a flier.

Many yachtsmen, unfortunately, tend to skimp on rafts, buying smaller models than they are likely to need and inspecting them

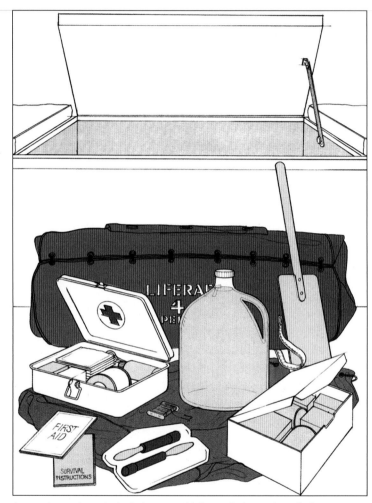

Arranged around a packed raft shown outside its seat locker are items for long-term survival—food (in the box at right), water, a fishing kit, an extra paddle, a first-aid kit and book, and flares *(center, bottom)*. Such equipment should be kept in a duffel bag and stowed with the raft. A crew abandoning ship should have a well-rehearsed plan for loading the raft with as much other gear as possible: flashlights, a Very pistol, a radio beacon, navigational equipment, as much extra food and water as can be stowed, blankets, and a change of clothing. Plastic bags for keeping equipment dry are also a good idea, as is reading matter; long hours at sea can be boring as well as frightening.

too infrequently. Size is important—every offshore skipper should have a raft large enough to accommodate the number of crew members he is likely to have aboard.

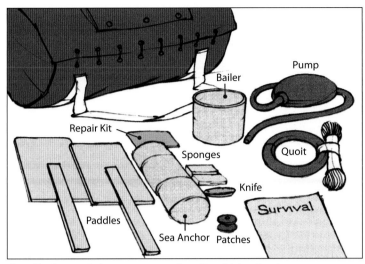

The self-inflating raft above comes prepackaged in a fabric valise that opens automatically upon inflation. Inside is a compact and ingenious collection of gear designed to ensure that the raft and its occupants can stay afloat until rescued.

The sailor above pitching a raft overboard has made fast the raft's painter, which is stowed inside a snap-fastened panel on the valise. A tug on the painter activates the CO_2 cartridge, automatically opening the valise and inflating the raft in 20 to 40 seconds.

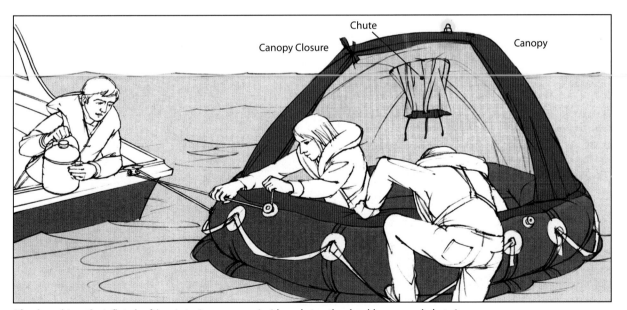

After launching, the inflated raft's painter is run around a cleat and back to the raft for quick release. Aided by lines on the raft's sides, a crewman climbs aboard. Contact with the water has activated two batteries underneath the raft that turn on lights inside and atop the closable canopy. A chute in the canopy top serves as an observation port and provides ventilation. When closed by a drawstring, it also functions as a reservoir, from which rain water can be drained.

Rescue by Air

When a disabled boat begins to founder, the skipper faces the grim necessity of leaving it. Long before this point, he should have called or signaled for help, and if his boat is radio equipped, he should have described any crew injuries. The Coast Guard and other rescue agencies still use boats close in, but today most evacuations at sea are made by helicopter. It is easier to pluck people from a vessel's deck than to transfer them from one boat to another.

Skipper and crew should wait aboard the craft as long as possible. People on a sinking boat are safer, more comfortable and easier to locate than people bobbing in the water. On arrival, the helicopter will hover low over the boat, its rotors creating a powerful downdraft. Therefore all rigging and lines must be secured so as not to hamper the rescue. When in position, the helicopter lowers a rescue basket to pick up people, one at a time.

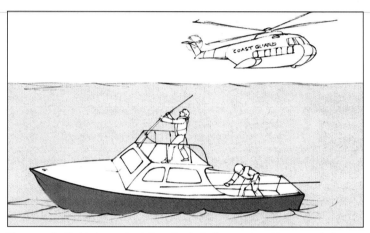

The crew of a disabled powerboat clears the decks for an approaching rescue helicopter by lowering the radio antenna and flagstaff. Radio contact should be maintained with the helicopter for as long as safely possible; because of close proximity, radioing can continue without the boat's antenna.

When the metal rescue basket is lowered, crew members should stand clear until it touches the deck. These baskets carry a heavy charge of static electricity built up by air friction against the whirring rotors, and only after the basket has reached the deck and released its charge is it safe to handle.

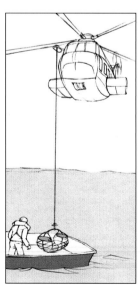

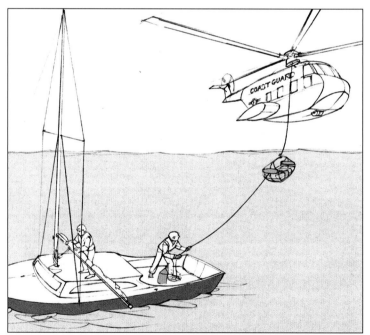

If kept from working close overhead by the mast of a sailboat, the helicopter drops a trail line weighted with a sandbag. While one crewman grabs the line, the other holds the boom clear. The helicopter then maneuvers to one side and lowers the rescue basket, which is hauled in with the trail line.

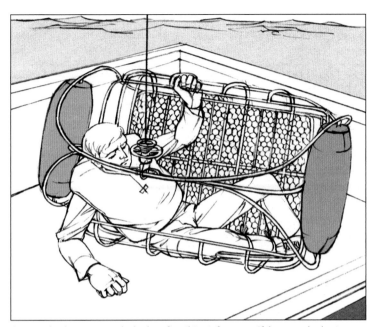

An injured sailor eases into the basket after tilting it for access. If the rescue basket is needed on another part of the boat, it can be unfastened; but the boat's crew should hold the loose line or let it dangle. The line must never be secured to the boat, lest the connection restrict the helicopter.

An overboard sailor swims to the rescue basket, which is held up by flotation devices. The sailor must enter quickly, since the rotors' wind whips up waves that can impede him. Because the basket is mostly submerged, the sailor can arrange himself inside while floating, before being lifted up.

Snug inside the rescue basket, the man being evacuated gives the thumbs-up signal, the sign that he is ready to be raised to the helicopter. He must be sure he is entirely inside the device before giving the signal or he risks falling out of the basket as it is drawn from the water. Once in the helicopter, the survivor should remain in the basket until instructed to leave—hatch doors may have to be closed before he can safely emerge.

When the Worst Happens

The Navy joins in the search and rescue efforts for a crewman that went overboard.

A Coast Guard helicopter rescues a sick passenger by lowering a stretcher.

Symbols, Saws, and Services

These pages contain a selection of information that will aid the sailor in understanding—and anticipating—the weather in his region. The symbols below are the most common ones used by meteorologists in generating the data upon which newspaper weather maps *(pages 26–27)* are based. On page 152 are the scientific underpinnings for some often reliable old saws about the weather. And the boxes on page 153 list radio frequencies and publications that provide useful data on tides, weather, etc.

Weather Map Symbols

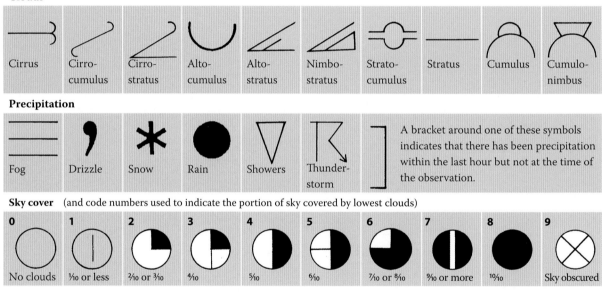

Clouds

| Cirrus | Cirro-cumulus | Cirro-stratus | Alto-cumulus | Alto-stratus | Nimbo-stratus | Strato-cumulus | Stratus | Cumulus | Cumulo-nimbus |

Precipitation

| Fog | Drizzle | Snow | Rain | Showers | Thunder-storm |

A bracket around one of these symbols indicates that there has been precipitation within the last hour but not at the time of the observation.

Sky cover   (and code numbers used to indicate the portion of sky covered by lowest clouds)

0	1	2	3	4	5	6	7	8	9
No clouds	1/10 or less	2/10 or 3/10	4/10	5/10	6/10	7/10 or 8/10	9/10 or more	10/10	Sky obscured

Barometric trend (past three hours)

Rising, then falling; now higher than—or the same as—three hours ago

Rising, then steady; or rising, then rising more slowly; now higher than three hours ago

Rising (steadily or unsteadily); now higher than three hours ago

Falling or steady, then rising; or rising, then rising faster; now higher than three hours ago

Steady; same as three hours ago

Falling, then rising; now lower than—or the same as—three hours ago

Falling, then steady; or falling, then falling more slowly; now lower than three hours ago

Falling (steadily or unsteadily); now lower than three hours ago

Steady or rising, then falling; or falling, then falling faster; now lower than three hours ago

Time of precipitation (by code numbers)

0	No precipitation	5	Four to five hours ago
1	Less than one hour ago	6	Five to six hours ago
2	One to two hours ago	7	Six to 12 hours ago
3	Two to three hours ago	8	More than 12 hours ago
4	Three to four hours ago	9	Unknown

Height of cloud base in feet (by code numbers)

0	0-149	5	2,000-3,499
1	150-299	6	3,500-4,999
2	300-599	7	5,000-6,499
3	600-999	8	6,500-7,999
4	1,000-1,999	9	above 8,000 or clear

Visibility

Numbers used to express visibility represent $\frac{1}{16}$ of a mile—e.g., a visibility of 8 = $\frac{8}{16}$, or $\frac{1}{2}$, mile.

When the Worst Happens

Weather Lore

Mackerel scales and mares' tails Make lofty ships carry short sails.	Cirrocumulus (mackerel scales) and cirrus (mares' tails) clouds are very often clues to the approach of a low-pressure storm system, which characteristically brings winds that would force mariners to shorten sail.
Glass high, heave short and away; Glass low, let your anchor stay.	The glass, or barometer, measures atmospheric pressure. When atmospheric pressure is high, the weather is generally clear and dry; but when atmospheric pressure is low, or falling, a storm is probably on its way.
When rain comes before the wind, Topsail sheets and halyards mind; When wind comes before the rain, Hoist your topsails up again.	In a low-pressure system, the first precipitation encountered is usually warm-front rain, followed by the strong winds associated with a following cold front. So, if warm-front rain comes first, cold-front winds will follow. However, if winds at the cold front come first and then rain, the low-pressure system is passing and lighter winds should follow.
Rain long foretold, long last; Short notice, soon past.	The slow-moving warm front sends a vanguard of gradually lowering and thickening clouds to announce its arrival; and when the warm front does arrive, it tends to stay for a day or more as it sluggishly passes over. A local thunderstorm, however, that forms with little warning will usually exhaust its energies in several hours.
Red sky at morning, Sailors take warning; Red sky at night, Sailors' delight.	A newly risen sun will give a reddish tint to low-lying, rain-bearing clouds—which may be part of a warm front in a low-pressure storm system. The sky will appear to be red at sunset when the blues and greens in the sun's rays are filtered out by the dust contained in the dry, high-pressure air of fair weather.
If smoke goes low, watch out for a blow; If smoke goes high, no rain comes by.	The high humidity of low-pressure air (and its stormy weather) will cause smoke to become heavy with moisture, and to sink. In the dry air of high pressure (and its fair weather), smoke particles will remain light, and will rise.
If mountains and cliffs in clouds appear, Some sudden and violent showers are near.	The first stage in the development of a thunderhead is the building up of a cumulus cloud. Thus, when clouds grow tall and begin to look like mountains and cliffs— especially over the shore on summer afternoons—a bad squall may be brewing.
At sunset with a cloud so black, A westerly wind you shall not lack.	In the Northern Hemisphere's band of prevailing westerlies, weather tends to move from west to east. Therefore, a black cloud at sunset may be part of a storm system moving in from the west. Because of the behavior of these winds around a low-pressure storm system, the passage of the system will be followed by winds out of the west to northwest.

Weather Broadcasts

The National Weather Service operates a network of VHF-FM radio stations that broadcast continuous bulletins. Updated every three to six hours, these forecasts usually cover local and regional weather— and marine conditions such as the tide and the height of waves in bays and coastal areas. Boat handlers can buy simple, battery-powered VHF-FM receivers that are designed solely to pick up these continuous broadcasts.

Skippers with VHF-FM marine radiotelephones can also receive these forecasts over the weather channels available on most sets. The reports are broadcast on two frequencies (identified by units known as megahertzes), 162.55 or 162.40, and they are specially designated on radiotelephone sets as weather channels WX-1 and WX-2 respectively. The former is the more common frequency, the latter being used when the broadcast range of one station overlaps that of another.

These stations have a range of 25 to 60 miles, depending on antenna height, quality of receiver and local terrain. But they do not, as yet, cover all American boating waters. To ascertain whether he is within range of a station, the boatman should obtain a *Marine Weather Services Chart* or *Coast Pilot* for his area. Both publications list the location of all stations.

In addition to the Weather Service's broadcasts, the boatman with a radiotelephone can listen to the Coast Guard reports of weather and sea conditions transmitted on regular channel 22. These transmissions from Coast Guard stations and lighthouses are a record of present conditions—not forecasts.

Publications for Mariners

The United States government publishes—and periodically updates—a number of publications and charts designed to help the boatman deal effectively with the two inevitable facts of his boating life: weather and water. Many of these documents are available from marine supply stores, and they also can be ordered directly from the government. A list of authorized sales agents, information on geographical areas covered, prices and orders can all be obtained by writing to: National Ocean Survey, Distribution Division (C44), 6501 Lafayette Avenue, Riverdale, Maryland 20840. Publications available include:

Tide Tables, published annually, contains predictions of the height and time of high and low tides. *Tidal Current Tables,* published annually, lists the speeds of tidal currents and the hours when these speeds occur. *Tidal Current Charts* graphically depicts the speed and direction of tidal currents in bays, harbors and sounds where landforms cause complex or unexpected flows. *Coast Pilots* and the *Great Lakes Pilot* include descriptions of local weather patterns—and any tides and currents. *Marine Weather Services Charts* include frequencies of radio stations that broadcast continuous weather reports, and locations of visual storm warnings.

For the dedicated weather watcher, the government publishes two periodicals: *Daily Weather Maps/Weekly Series* shows the actual weather recorded in the United States the previous week, and *Average Monthly Outlook* gives a 30-day forecast. Both are available by subscription from: Superintendent of Documents, Government Printing Office, Washington, D.C. 20402.

When the Worst Happens

Glossary

Battens. Flexible strips of wood or fiberglass placed in a sail to help the leech retain its proper shape.

Becket. A loop, eye or grommet; the eye in the strap of a block to which a line can be attached.

Belay. To secure a line, usually to a cleat.

Bend. To fasten, as a sail to the mast; to tie two ropes together or to tie a line to an anchor; a knot by which an end of one rope is tied to another to lengthen it.

Bight. An open loop in a rope; a bend in a coastline forming a bay.

Bilge. The area of a boat inside the hull and near the bottom—usually beneath floorboards.

Bitt. A single or double post fixed on a deck for securing mooring lines and tow-lines. On a dock a bitt is more commonly called a bollard.

Bitter end. The free end of a rope.

Block. A wood or metal shell enclosing one or more sheaves, through which lines are led.

Boom vang. A single line—usually wire—or a block and tackle commonly used to hold down the boom while reaching or running.

Broach. To allow a boat to swerve and heel dangerously, especially in a following sea, so that the boat turns broadside to the waves and is in danger of capsizing or foundering.

Buntlines. Wire ropes on square-riggers used to haul a sail up to its yard before men go aloft to furl.

Cable. A heavy rope or chain commonly used for towing or mooring large vessels.

Capstan. A vertical drum, revolving on a spindle, used for hoisting or hauling.

Car. A metal fitting that slides on a track and to which blocks are attached.

Cast off. To let go mooring or docking lines; to remove the turns of a line from a cleat; to untie a knot.

Center of lateral resistance. The hypothetical point below a boat's waterline at which the vessel can be pushed sideways through the water without turning.

Chafing gear. A covering put around a short section of line to reduce wear, or on the rigging to protect the sails.

Chain plate. A narrow metal plate attached to the hull as a fastening point for shrouds and stays.

Chock. A metal fitting, usually mounted on or in a boat's rail, to guide hawsers or lines for mooring or towing.

Cleat. A wood or metal fitting with two projecting horns fastened to some part of the boat, to which a line is belayed.

Clew. The lower, after corner of a sail where the foot meets the leech.

Coil. To gather a rope in circular turns for ease in handling and storage.

Comber. A wave, usually large, that breaks over a considerable distance.

Countercurrent. A current flowing in a direction opposite to that of another current.

Cringle. A circular eye, often formed by a metal ring, grommet or piece of rope worked into the eye, set in the corners or on the edges of a sail and used for fastening the sail to spars or running rigging.

Dorade ventilator. A deck box with cowl and internal arrangement that allows air but not water to enter the cabin.

Downhaul. A length of wire or line that pulls down the tack of the sail or the foremost end of the boom to tighten the luff.

Drag. To draw or trail an anchor along the bottom when the anchor fails to hold; the force that acts on the rudder in a direction perpendicular to that of a boat's course.

Drift. The speed, in knots, of a current.

Ease. To slack off, slack away.

Ebb. The tidal movement of water away from the land and toward the sea, as in ebb current; the falling of the water level from high tide to low tide, as in ebb tide. Colloquially, ebb tide is used to refer to the movements of both current and water level.

Eye. A loop in a rope that has been seized, spliced or knotted.

Fairlead. A metal, plastic or wooden eye—usually attached to a deck—that guides a line in a desired direction.

Fake. To coil back and forth in loops so the line is free for running; to fold a sail back and forth when furling.

Fall. The hauling end or section of a line in a tackle; the line that makes up the tackle.

Fetch. The distance along open water or land over which the wind blows; to head toward or achieve a desired destination under sail, particularly with an adverse wind or tide.

Flood. The movement of water toward the land and away from the sea; the rising of the water level from low tide to high tide.

Foot. The bottom edge of a sail.

Foul weather gear. Rain gear worn on board in bad weather. Traditionally called oilskins because in former days cotton jackets and trousers were waterproofed with linseed oil. Modern foul weather gear is usually of nylon coated with a plastic skin.

Freeboard. The vertical distance measured on the boat's side from the water-line to the deck.

Front. An area or line of temperature disparity between a warm air mass and a cold air mass, as in cold front, warm front.

Furl. To roll, fold or wrap. close to—or around—something, as in furling a sail or flag.

Gale. A range of winds from 28 to 47 knots.

Ground tackle. A general term for the anchor, anchor rodes and various fittings used for securing a vessel at anchor.

Halyard. A line to hoist and lower a sail.

Handy-billy. A small tackle.

Hank. One of the fittings that attaches the luff of a headsail and a staysail to a stay.

Hawser. A heavy line or cable five inches or more in circumference used on large vessels for mooring or towing.

Head. The top corner of a triangular sail; a seagoing lavatory.

Heave to. The general term for various methods of riding out a storm without attempting to travel through it; to lie almost stationary while still underway by heading up into the wind, by adjusting engine speed or by trimming the sails in such a way that the boat will head up and then fall off the wind.

Heaving line. A light line, usually attached to a docking line or other heavier object, used for throwing across an open stretch of water. After being caught, a heaving line is used to haul the heavier object across the water.

Hitch. A method for securing a line to an object or to another line that is inert.

Hurricane. A wind of 64 knots or more; a tropical cyclone with extremely high winds.

Jigger. The mizzen of a yawl or ketch. Formerly, the sail aft of the mizzen on ships with four masts or more.

Jury-rig. A temporary or makeshift rig set up to substitute for some broken or lost piece of equipment.

Knot. Broadly, any intentional and firm interweaving of rope or ropes; specifically, a knot is formed when a rope is turned back onto itself and tied, such as a bowline. A nautical mile equal in distance to one minute of latitude (and 1.15 statute miles); a common contraction for speed expressed in nautical miles per hour.

Land breeze. A breeze that blows off the land toward the water. Also called an offshore breeze.

Lash. To tie down an object, or secure one object to another with line.

Lay. The direction in which the strands of a rope are twisted, usually right-handed or clockwise. In hard-laid rope the strands are tightly twisted; in soft-laid rope the strands are more nearly parallel.

Lazarette. A space for stowage in a boat's stern.

Lead. When pronounced "leed," the direction of a line; when pronounced "led," the weight at the end of a line used for taking soundings.

Lee helm. The tendency of a boat to steer off or away from the wind, usually due to an improperly balanced sail plan.

Leech. The after edge of a sail.

Leeway. The lateral movement of a ship caused by the force of the wind.

Limber holes. Notches cut into a boat's frames near the keel to allow bilge water to run to the lowest point in the hull.

Line. A general term for a piece of rope designated for a specific use on board a boat. Sheets and halyards, for example, are lines.

Luff. The leading edge of a sail; the fluttering of a sail when the boat is pointed too close to the wind or the sail is let out too far.

Make fast. To secure a line to an object; to doubly secure a cleated—or otherwise tied—line by means of an added hitch.

Marline. Two-stranded nautical twine.

Mayday. An international radiotelephone signal word (from *m'aider,* French for "help me") used as a distress call.

Mean high water. The average level of high tide for any area.

Mean low water. The average level of low tide for any area.

Messenger line. A light line, like a heaving line, used to haul heavy lines.

Mizzen. The sail set on the mizzenmast; the aftermast of a yawl or ketch.

Mooring. A fixed anchor or weight by which a boat is kept at a permanent berth; the place in which a boat can be moored.

Neap tide. A tide of less than average range, occurring at the first and third quarters of the moon.

Outhaul. A fitting on the boom to which the sail's clew is attached, and by means of which the foot of the sail is stretched out along the boom.

Override. One turn of line that accidentally settles over another around a winch or capstan.

Painter. A bow line for a small boat.

Pitchpole. To somersault, as when a boat is thrown end over end by a wave.

Purchase. A tackle, usually permanently rigged, and used most often for main-sheets.

Quarter. Either side of a boat's stern; to sail with the wind on the quarter.

Ratlines. Sections of wood or rope that are fastened between the shrouds of a square-rigger in a ladder-like fashion to allow the crew to climb aloft.

Reef. To reduce sail area without removing the sail entirely, by partially lowering the sail and securing loose fabric along the foot with lines called reef points.

Reeve. To pass the end of a line through a hole or opening, as through a block or a fairlead.

Riding turns. A second layer of turns wrapped over a seizing or whipping; also known as riders.

Rigging. The lines or wires fitted to spars and sails for support and control. Standing rigging is made up of the fixed shrouds and stays that provide lateral and longitudinal support to the spars. Running rigging comprises the halyards, sheets, tackles, outhauls and downhauls to put up, take down and adjust sail.

Rode. An anchor line.

Scope. The ratio between the length of an anchor rode and the depth of the water in which a vessel is anchored.

Sea anchor. A bulky device, frequently a conical canvas bag, thrown overboard and dragged astern to hold a boat's bow into the wind and sea.

Sea breeze. A breeze blowing off the water toward the land. Also called an onshore breeze.

Seacock. A shutoff valve attached to through-hull pipes.

Seize. To bind two ropes together or bind a rope to another object.

Set. The direction in which a current is moving.

Shackle. A U-shaped metal fitting with a cross pin or clevis pin that fits across the opening of the U as a closure.

Sheave. The grooved wheel in a block, or in a masthead fitting or elsewhere, over which a line runs. (Pronounced shiv.)

Sheet. A line used to trim a sail.

Shrouds. Ropes or wires led from the mast to chain plates at deck level on either side of the mast, and which hold the mast from falling or bending sideways.

Small craft advisory. A warning (either verbal or visual) issued by the Coast Guard or other authority to alert boatmen to potentially hazardous weather or sea conditions.

Snatch block. A block hinged on one side and latched on the other so that it can be opened to receive the bight of a line and then closed to hold the line securely.

Snub. To quickly check, by cleating or other means, a line that is running out.

Spar. General term for any wood or metal pole—mast, boom, yard, gaff or sprit—used to carry and give shape to sails.

Spring line. A long docking line rigged to limit a boat's fore and aft motion, usually run from a boat's stern to a point well forward, and from the bow well aft.

Spring tide. A tide of greater than average range, occurring around the times of new and full moon.

Squall. A sudden violent wind, often accompanied by rain or snow.

Squall line. A line of thunderstorms—sometimes hundreds of miles long—accompanied by extremely high winds.

Standing part. The inactive part of a rope, often near the midsection.

Stay. A rope or wire running forward or aft from the mast to support it. The headstay is the foremost stay on which the jib is set; a forestay is aft of the headstay and carries a staysail; the backstay offsets the pull of the headstay.

Steadying sail. A small sail used to lessen the roll of a motorboat in beam or following seas.

Stop. To tie down a furled sail; a rope or cloth strip used for that purpose; a temporary tie made with twine around a furled sail, especially a spinnaker, and designed to be broken out by a hard pull on the sheet so that the sail will fill.

Storm. A range of winds of from 48 to 63 knots; the generic term for severe foul weather.

Stove in. A boat broken in from outside is said to be stove in.

Swage. A cylindrical metal shank cold-rolled onto the end of a wire as a terminal.

Swell. A wave, or succession of waves—originally generated by winds—that have left their area of generation and have moved into areas of weaker wind, and are decreasing in height. Swells are fairly regular in length and height, and have rounded crests.

Tackle. An arrangement of lines reeved through blocks to provide mechanical advantage for hoisting or hauling. (Pronounced TAY-kel.)

Take a turn. To pass a line once around an object.

Thimble. A grooved round or teardrop-shaped metal or plastic fitting spliced into an eye of rope or wire to prevent chafe and distortion of the eye.

Tidal current. The horizontal movement of water caused by the ebbing and flooding of the tide.

Tidal range. The amount of change in an area's water level from low tide to high tide; e.g., an area covered by two feet of water at low tide and six feet of water at high tide has a tidal range of four feet.

Topping lift. A halyard attached to the spinnaker pole that is raised or lowered to keep the spinnaker properly trimmed; a line from the masthead to the end of the main boom to support the boom.

Topsides. The upper part of a boat's sides from the designed waterline up to the rail.

Total center of effort. The geometrical center of a sail plan.

Track. A metal strip attached to a spar or a deck to accommodate sail slides, cars or blocks.

Trysail. Small sail of heavy cloth set in place of the mainsail during heavy winds.

Turnbuckle. An adjustable fastening for attaching the standing rigging to the chain plates, and for adjusting the tension on the standing rigging.

Turning block. A block fixed on deck and used to alter the direction of a line by as much as 180°. A small turning block is often called a cheek block.

Unlay. To open up or separate the strands of a rope.

Veer. To pay out, or let out, chain or line.

Warps. Heavy lines trailed overboard to create drag when running before a following sea in exceptionally bad weather. To warp is to move a boat from one place to another by hauling on a warp, or line, attached to a fixed object.

Weather helm. The tendency of a boat to steer up or toward the wind, usually due to an improperly balanced sail plan.

Whip. To bind the end of a rope with twine to keep it from fraying.

Winch. A device with a revolving drum around which a line may be turned in order to provide mechanical advantage in hoisting or hauling.

Windlass. A special form of winch, with a horizontally mounted drum, commonly used on pleasure boats to hoist an anchor.

Working end. The fastened or manipulated end of a rope.

Yard. A horizontal spar from which a sail is set on a square-rigger.

Index

Index

Index

159

Boat Maintenance
The Complete Guide to Keeping Your Boat ShipShape
By Skills Institute Press
Learn how to properly maintain a boat for years of trouble-free, smooth sailing.
ISBN: 978-1-56523-549-6
$19.95 • 160 Pages

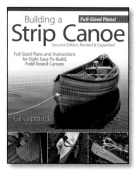

Building a Strip Canoe, 2nd Edition
Full-Sized Plans and Instructions for Eight Easy-To-Build, Field-Tested Canoes
By Gil Gilpatrick
Paddle along with an expert outdoorsman and canoe builder as he shares his experience in guiding both novice and accomplished woodworkers in building a canoe with easy step-by-step instructions.

ISBN: 978-1-56523-483-3
$24.95 • 112 Pages

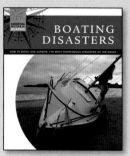

Boating Disasters
How to Avoid, and Survive, the Most Horrendous Disasters on the Water
By Skills Institute Press
ISBN: 978-1-56523-590-8

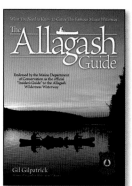

The Allagash Guide
What You Need to Know to Canoe this Famous Maine Waterway
By Gil Gilpatrick
A book so extensively detailed about canoeing the Allagash River in Maine, by expert outdoorsman Gil Gilpatrick, it's like having him along for the trip.
ISBN: 978-1-56523-488-8
$11.95 • 104 Pages

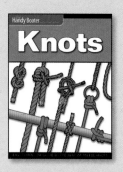

Knots
Easy-to-Follow Guide to the 30 Most Useful Knots
By Skills Institute Press
ISBN: 978-1-56523-589-2

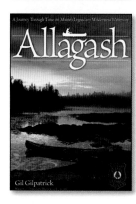

Allagash
A Journey Through Time on Maine's Legendary Wilderness Waterway
By Gil Gilpatrick
Take a journey down the awe-inspiring Allagash River with Gil Gilpatrick as he skillfully weaves historic facts and speculative fiction into fascinating stories about this legendary waterway.
ISBN: 978-1-56523-487-1
$19.95 • 232 pages